GERONIMO
WOLF OF THE WARPATH

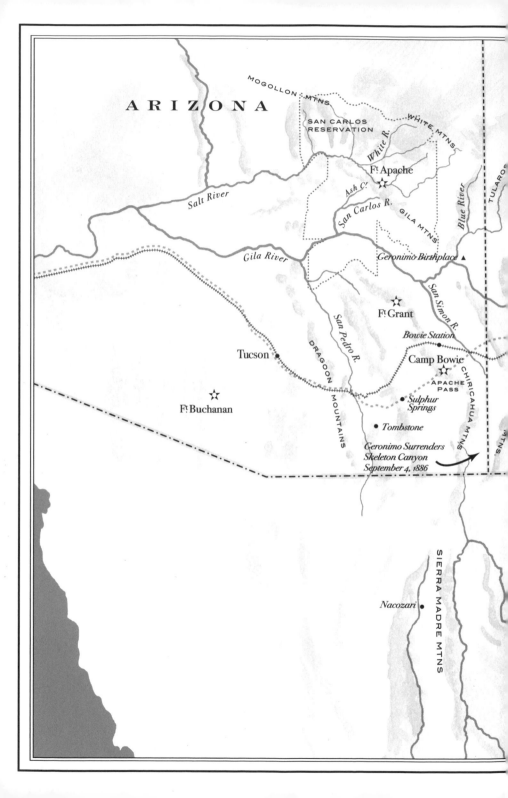

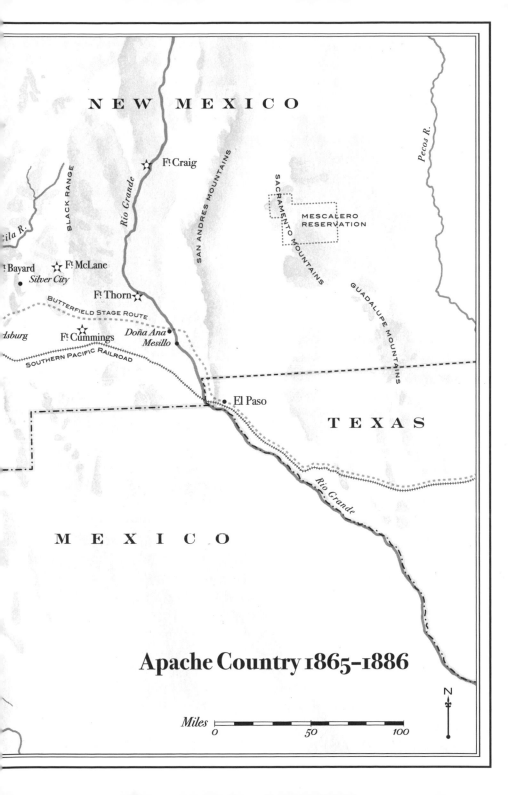

NEW MEXICO

☆ Ft Craig

BLACK RANGE

Rio Grande

SAN ANDRES MOUNTAINS

SACRAMENTO MOUNTAINS

Pecos R.

MESCALERO
RESERVATION

Gila R.

Bayard ☆ Ft McLane

Silver City

Ft Thorn ☆

GUADALUPE MOUNTAINS

BUTTERFIELD STAGE ROUTE

sburg ☆ Ft Cummings

Doña Ana
Mesillo

SOUTHERN PACIFIC RAILROAD

El Paso

TEXAS

MEXICO

Rio Grande

Apache Country 1865–1886

N

Miles
0   50   100

Geronimo

GERONIMO
WOLF OF THE WARPATH

RALPH MOODY

STERLING PUBLISHING CO., INC.
New York

A FLYING POINT PRESS BOOK

Design: PlutoMedia
Front cover photograph: Edward S. Curtis, courtesy of Northwestern University
Frontispiece photograph: National Archives

Library of Congress Cataloging-in-Publication Data Available

2 4 6 8 10 9 7 5 3 1

Published by Sterling Publishing Co., Inc.
387 Park Avenue South, New York, NY 10016
Original edition published by Random House, Inc.
Copyright © 1958 by Charles Moody and Edna Morales
New material in this updated edition
Copyright © 2006 by Flying Point Press
Maps copyright © by Richard Thompson, Creative Freelancers, Inc.
Distributed in Canada by Sterling Publishing
c/o Canadian Manda Group, 165 Dufferin Street
Toronto, Ontario, Canada M6K 3H6
Distributed in the United Kingdom by GMC Distribution Services
Castle Place, 166 High Street, Lewes, East Sussex, England BN7 1XU
Distributed in Australia by Capricorn Link (Australia) Pty. Ltd.
P.O. Box 704, Windsor, NSW 2756, Australia

Sterling ISBN-13: 978-1-4027-3612-4
ISBN-10: 1-4027-3612-6

For information about custom editions, special sales, premium and
corporate purchases, please contact Sterling Special Sales
Department at 800-805-5489 or specialsales@sterlingpub.com.

CONTENTS

CHAPTER 1

APACHES

"APACHE! APACHE!" FOR NEARLY THREE HUNDRED years before the first Americans made their way into the Southwest, this cry had brought terror to the hearts of the Mexicans.

Soon after Columbus discovered America, Spanish soldiers came to the New World in search of treasure. They conquered the Aztecs of Mexico, robbed their golden cities and seized their rich mines. Not long afterwards the Spaniards heard stories of other golden cities far to the north. These were said to be the Seven Cities of Cibola, so rich that even the streets were paved with gold. The Spanish believed these stories. In 1540 Coronado led his forces into the deserts of what are now our states of

Arizona and New Mexico to find and plunder the golden cities.

Coronado found no gold but discovered a tribe of friendly Indians with unbelievable strength and endurance. He was angry at having found no gold, but here was just the kind of labor the Spanish needed for their mines in Mexico. Hundreds of Indians were captured, chained together and driven south as slaves.

With guns and armor against the stone-tipped spears and arrows of the naked Indians, the Spanish had little trouble in capturing slaves. But they had made a bad mistake. These Indians of the desert had not only the endurance of the wolf but the cunning of the fox, the courage of the panther and the fierceness of the wildcat. When they saw their tribesmen tortured and driven away as slaves, their friendliness turned to hatred. They determined that every Spaniard should be killed.

The Aztecs had been conquered because they tried to fight the Spanish soldiers in open battles. These Indians of the desert were far too intelligent for that. They realized quickly that open battles gave all the advantage to soldiers with guns and armor. They also realized that the advantage would be their own if they stalked their enemy as wild beasts stalked their prey: a sudden rush from hiding, a lightning-fast kill, and a quick escape if the odds were against them.

As the years went by, the Spaniards and many of

their descendants, the Mexicans, grew wealthy. Great ranches with thousands of horses and cattle filled the fertile valleys of Mexico. Villages sprang up, stores were opened, and long trains of pack mules carried bright-colored cloth, wine, food, guns and household goods to the villages.

As the Mexicans spread farther toward the north, the Indians of the desert were not idle. Like the hunting beasts of their homeland, they waited patiently for their prey to come closer. But as they waited they prepared for war. Every boy in his teens was trained as a warrior. The women and children were taught to scatter and hide in case of attack.

When all was in readiness, the Indians of the desert struck. Small raiding parties slipped southward across arid deserts and through rugged mountain canyons. Moving like shadows through the moonlight, they would creep up and lie hidden around the buildings of a lonely Mexican ranch.

In the first gray light of dawn a bloodcurdling war whoop would rip through the stillness. As the startled rancher and his men grabbed up their guns and ran out to defend their families, they were cut down from ambush by stone-tipped arrows. If the Mexicans tried to defend their homes from within, the buildings were set afire and the victims killed as they ran from the flames. Before word of the massacre could be taken to nearest village and the soldiers alerted, the Indians were far away—back in the deserts and mountains of their homeland.

At first the raids were made only for revenge, to kill the hated enemy who had stolen and enslaved their tribesmen. Soon, though, the Indians learned the value of everything the Mexicans had. Indian women and children like bright-colored clothes, flour, corn meal, sugar and household pots and pans. Horses were good to ride, and beef was better to eat than coyote or antelope. But it was guns, ammunition and knives that caught the warriors' eyes. The raids were no longer for revenge alone, but for plunder. And there was more plunder to be had from the villages and pack trains than from the ranches.

After the Indian raids began, the Mexicans started to keep large companies of cavalry at their villages. But the Indians quickly learned how to deal with them. Suddenly, in the stillness just before dawn, a whooping, howling band of mounted Indians would race into a sleeping village. Before the echo of their war whoop had died away, a house would be set afire and a few horses stampeded away from the village herd. As the mounted Indians streaked away toward the north, driving the stolen horses before them, the cavalrymen would leap from their beds, saddle their mounts and race in pursuit. Still whooping and howling, the Indians would keep just out of range of the soldiers' guns, leading them farther and farther away from the village.

With the soldiers barely out of sight and hearing, and with the villagers frantically fighting fire, the dreaded war whoop rose again from every direction. Indians leaped from hiding with spears raised and bows drawn tight. Before the bewildered villagers could run for their firearms the massacre was over. Stores and houses were stripped of everything an Indian could use. Cattle, horses and mules were rounded up and their backs loaded with the plunder. Then the torch was carried from house to house. As the village went up in flames, the Indians scattered and headed back for their homeland, each one driving a heavily loaded animal or two.

Meanwhile, the mounted warriors led the Mexican cavalrymen far out into the waterless, brush-covered desert. When the horses were nearly exhausted, the Indians scattered like blown leaves, each warrior slipping to the ground and crouching behind a clump of brush with an arrow to his bowstring. If the soldiers were foolish enough to scatter and hunt them, stone-tipped arrows picked them out of their saddles one by one.

Without a drop of water these desert Indians could run all day through the burning heat. But an exhausted horse or a soldier with a dry canteen would die of thirst and sunstroke within a few hours. If the chase had been a long one the Indians didn't bother to hunt down and kill the Mexican cavalrymen, the desert would take care of that.

Soon the desert Indians became the most dreaded

enemy of the Mexicans. The sound of their war whoop brought terror to every village, every ranch, and to every caravan on the trails. The Maricopa Indians were the Mexicans' friends and in their language the word for enemy sounded like *apache*. Soon the Mexicans were calling these raiding Indians from the desert Apaches, and the *Apaches* well earned the name.

One by one the ranches and settlements on the frontier were abandoned. The Mexicans moved farther and farther back to the south, but the raiding Apaches followed them. The Mexican government greatly increased the number of soldiers, but they could not cope with the sudden Apache attacks. How could they fight an enemy which would not face them in battle, which could never be discovered until it attacked, and which scattered like blown leaves if pursued?

By the time the first American frontiersmen came into the Southwest, Apache women and children were dressed in bright-colored Mexican clothing, and the warriors were well equipped with stolen guns, ammunition and war ponies. The Mexican government was finding it so hard to recruit soldiers that, in desperation, it set bounties on Apache scalps. It would pay one hundred dollars in gold for an Apache warrior's scalp, fifty dollars for a woman's and twenty-five dollars for a child's.

But this caused even greater trouble. In offering bounties for scalps, the Mexicans made a worse mistake than the Spanish did when they took the first Apache slaves. The Apaches had never scalped their victims, but when they learned of the Mexican bounties their hatred and anger flared like a raging fire. If the Mexicans were going to make torture and cruelty a part of warfare, the Apaches would show them the true meaning of the words. A few Apache scalps were taken by Mexicans, but every act of cruelty was repaid ten times over by the Indians.

CHAPTER 2

GOKLIYA

IN JUNE 1829, AN APACHE BOY WAS BORN IN A DEEP canyon near the headwaters of the Gila River. The place is situated on what is now the state line between Arizona and New Mexico. He was a sleepy, quiet baby and his mother named him Gokliya, which in the Apache language means "He Who Yawns." But as Geronimo this sleepy baby was to become the most famous of all the Apaches.

Gokliya's father had married into the most northern of the nine Apache tribes, but his grandfather was Maco, chief of the tribe that lived farthest to the south. Maco's warriors were the fiercest of all the Apaches, and he was the most feared leader of raids against the Mexicans.

The Apaches had no written language and no schools. But the grandson of a great chief could not be allowed to grow up in ignorance, because one day he himself would probably be a chief. First, though, he must prove himself the most brilliant warrior among his tribesmen—the bravest, the most tireless, the best hunter and the most convincing speaker in the council of warriors.

When Gokliya was old enough to walk, his father began training him. Every day they played together for hours. But every game was a lesson—something to prepare the child to become a great chief. A game they played more than any other was hide-and-seek. By the time Gokliya was two years old he had become so cunning at the game that he could hide from his mother within a few steps of the wikiup (a wikiup is the name for an Apache's house—it is usually made of wood stakes covered with animal skins and can be taken down and moved easily). With his red-brown naked body curled into a round ball, he could lie as still as the red-brown boulders that lay scattered on the desert around him. It would take a sharper eye than a Mexican's to see that he was a boy instead of a boulder.

For hours at a time Gokliya and his father would trace the almost invisible track of the kangaroo rat, until at last they trailed it to its hole beneath a mesquite bush. With every tracing Gokliya's eye grew keener, his legs stronger, and his body toughened to stand the scorching heat of the desert sun.

Sometimes they would play follow-the-leader, always at a trot. Gokliya's father would lead the way over the rockiest ground, through gulches, thickets of thorn bush and beds of cactus. Gokliya's bare feet were often cut by sharp stones and his skin was scratched by thorns until it bled. But his father gave him no sympathy. A boy must learn to bear pain without complaining.

By the time Gokliya was five, the games would cover six or seven miles over the roughest part of the desert. If he lagged behind, his father trotted on and left him to follow as best he could. For a boy who was to be a future chief must learn never to give up because he was tired. He was never allowed to have a drop of water when he and his father were playing, but was taught to carry a pebble in his mouth to keep the saliva flowing. With every game Gokliya's endurance increased. He learned to pay no attention to weariness, heat, pain or thirst. His body became slim, his muscles springy, and the soles of his feet as tough as leather.

When Gokliya was six his father taught him to chip flint and make his own spear and bow and arrows. These were no playthings such as most white boys make. Hours of work were put into the careful chipping of each spear or arrowhead. When a mistake was made the stone was thrown away and the long job started all over. The straightest grained ash wood had to be found for arrow shafts, and each one scraped with a sharp stone until it was perfectly round. The bow was made of the toughest hickory and scraped until its spring was equal to the strength of Gokliya's arm. The bowstring was a tough sinew from the leg of an antelope.

At first all of Gokliya's shooting of arrows and throwing of spears was done at the trunk of a tree. Day after day he and his father spent hours at shooting and spear throwing. As the months went by Gokliya grew and his arm strengthened. His father showed him how to stick rawhide to the face of his bow with glue made from a boiled deer hoof. This gave the bow a greater spring and made the arrows fly faster and farther. The spears were tipped with heavier heads, to make them carry farther and cut deeper into the trunk of a tree.

From early boyhood Gokliya was quick, restless, and determined to outdo the other boys of his age. As soon as he was able to make his arrows hit the target, he was anxious to go with his father when he hunted deer. "No, my son," his father told him, "it will be many summers before you are strong enough to hunt the deer or smart enough to hunt the antelope."

"I am already strong and smart," Gokliya answered. "I can shoot my arrows farther than the other boys and I can follow the trail of a kangaroo rat when they cannot find a footprint."

His father laughed. "You are a great hunter, but you are a very little one. Before you hunt the deer your arm must be as strong as mine. From thirty paces you must be able to bury an arrowhead out of sight in the trunk of a tree. First you must learn to hunt the rat and the rabbit."

"I could hunt them now if you would let me," Gokliya shouted angrily. "Can I not hit a tree that is no bigger around than a rat?"

"Patience! Patience, my son!" his father told him. "A hunter needs patience more than he needs a strong arm and a sharp eye. The one without it comes home with his belly as empty as the foolish coyote that chases after swallows. No boy who shouts at his father is ready to be a hunter."

All Apache boys wanted to become hunters and warriors, but none was so determined as Gokliya. And when Gokliya was determined he let nothing stand in his way. Hour after hour, day after day, he practiced with his bow and spears. Anger always rose quickly in him, but he forced himself to bite his tongue when he wanted to shout at his father or mother. Before he was eleven years old he could shoot one arrow after another into a slender tree at a distance of thirty paces, and he had not shouted at his parents in months. It was then that his father took him on his first hunt.

CHAPTER 3

THE FIRST KILL

THE MORNING STAR WAS FADING WHEN GOKLIYA'S FATHER touched him lightly on the arm. Naked and wide-awake the boy sprang from the deerskin in which he slept. Quickly he snatched up his bow and arrows, following his father out of the wikiup.

Gokliya's first hunt was to be for desert rats, the little animals that look like tiny kangaroos and live in brush-covered parts of the desert. From trailing them he had long ago learned where their villages were. Proudly he trotted close at his father's heels. Over his shoulder he carried a little quiver of arrows, and in his hand his best bow. His heart thumped against his ribs, and his blood ran hot as he thought of making his first kill. He only wished his father would trot faster.

The sun had not yet risen when Gokliya's father stopped. He whispered, "The rat, he is breakfast for the coyote and the fox. He likes to hunt his own breakfast at sunup, but he has learned to be afraid and careful. If he hears one little sound he will not come out of his hole." Dropping to the ground, he crept toward a clump of bushes that covered a rat village.

Gokliya dropped flat behind his father and wriggled forward. As they neared the clump he whipped an arrow from his quiver and strung it to his bow. The arrows rattled together and the bowstring twanged. His father turned his head and scowled, then lay motionless. Gokliya squirmed up beside him and tried to lie just as still. He held his bow half sprung in front of his face, with an arrow tight against the bowstring.

Gokliya and his father lay behind a little patch of brush not more than a foot high. Scattered around them on the desert stood high bushes. Not more than ten paces in front of them was the large clump that covered the rat village. As he peered through the low brush Gokliya could see half a dozen holes, no bigger around than his own fist. These led down to the underground village. His hand tightened on the bow, and his eyes sparkled as he watched for a head to pop up from one of the holes.

There was no breeze, and the desert was as still as if there were no living thing upon it. But to Gokliya the beating of his own heart sounded like a racing pony's hoofs. Slowly the gray of morning changed to a golden glow as the sun rose. The boy's neck arched as a result of his lying with his muscles tense and his head held high. His eyes burned from staring unblinkingly at the rat holes. Beside him his father lay as if he were asleep. Every muscle and nerve was relaxed. His chin rested on his arm and his eyes were half closed, but they saw everything around him.

The climbing sun became hot on Gokliya's back, and his arms ached from holding the arrow tight against his bowstring. He was sure he had not looked away from the rat holes for a second, yet he had seen nothing. This hunting business wasn't as exciting as he had expected, and he began to understand what his father had told him about a hunter's needing patience. He was thinking about these things when he felt a slight pressure from his father's elbow. As he glanced around he saw his father eyes fixed on one corner of the brush clump. When he looked there himself he saw the shine of two beady eyes, a little head pushed cautiously from a hole, looking this way and that.

Excitement swept over Gokliya like a flame. He sprang to his knees and yanked his bowstring tight. Before the arrow could take wing, the rat's head had snapped back into the hole. The shot was a bad one. The arrow kicked up a shower of sand at least a foot away from the hole, then clattered on through the dry leaves and twigs of the brush clump.

Gokliya knew he had been wrong in springing to his knees, and he was ashamed of the bad shot he had made, but his father said nothing. Apaches never spanked or struck their children, and seldom scolded them. As Gokliya drew another arrow from his quiver and fitted it to his bowstring, his father's hand reached out quietly for them. Without a word he laid them on the ground at arm's length beyond his head, then seemed to go back to sleep.

The sun rose higher and the sand grew hot, but Gokliya's father lay as if he were dead. No leaf stirred, no beady eyes glistened in the blackness of a rat hole, and no little head poked out to peer about. Gokliya tried to copy his father. He lay with his body relaxed, his chin on his arm and his eyes half closed. He tried not to let his attention wander from the rat holes, but the heat and stillness made him drowsy. Once, when he was sure he had only winked, his eyes came open to see a rat half out of its hole and peering around nervously.

Gokliya was sure his father was asleep and had not seen the rat. His first thought was to call out or shake him, but he had learned well from his first mistake. He turned his eyes toward his father and found him very much awake. One arm was extended to grasp the bow, and the other held the arrow tightly against the bowstring.

Gokliya was impatient for his father to shoot before the rat should duck back into the hole, but the warrior's only sign of life was his bright black eyes, now wide open and watching. For several minutes the little kangaroo waited, half out of its hole, listening and watching for any movement. Then it darted to another clump of brush, streaking across the sand in quick, bounding leaps and diving out of sight.

A few minutes later another head appeared from another hole above the village. This rat stopped only to look and listen for a moment, then skittered across the sand to join the first one. Gokliya's father still lay motionless, but the boy's heart was pounding again with excitement. He had to bite his tongue to keep from crying out, and it took every bit of his will power to hold his body still.

One after another, half a dozen rats came up from the village, stopped for a moment to peer about, then bounded away to some clump of bushes near by. It was then that Gokliya saw his father's arm draw the bowstring slowly and tightly. As the boy looked in the direction toward which the arrow pointed, he saw that one of the rats was sitting up on its hind legs, eating something that it held in its fore paws. There was a hissing sound as the arrow leaped away, a light twang of the bowstring, then all was still again. The rat lay motionless, pinned to the ground by the arrow.

Gokliya's heart leaped, but he forced his body to lie as quietly as if he were asleep. Slowly his father pushed the bow back within his reach, and just as slowly and carefully Gokliya fitted another arrow to the string.

This time the wait was not long. The kill had been so noiseless that the other feeding rats had been startled only for a moment. Soon they were bounding from bush to bush in search of their delayed breakfast. Straight across the little sandy opening in front of Gokliya a hopping rat stopped, picked up something from among the leaves and sat nibbling it. The boy's fist tightened on the bow. His fingers pinched hard against the shaft of the arrow, drawing the string back until the arrowhead was nearly at his fist. His mouth was dry, and his eyes burned as he sighted at his first living target. But there was no tremble in his hand or arm. He scarcely heard the twang of his own bowstring or the hiss of his arrow. This time his aim was good and his arrow flew fast and true.

Gokliya wanted to jump and shout from the excitement of his first kill but, above everything, he was determined to be a great hunter and warrior. His father had not made a sound or a move when his arrow had killed, so Gokliya made himself lie still. His hand was reaching cautiously for another arrow when his father rose and said, "It is well, little one! Now bring your kill! We go to show Mother that her son is a great hunter."

CHAPTER 4

GOKLIYA THE BRAGGER

ONLY THE RAT THAT GOKLIYA HAD SHOT WAS TAKEN back, and he trotted proudly behind his father, carrying it. Going to the hunt had seemed to take forever, but the return seemed short, because Gokliya's head was busier than his legs.

Among the Apaches an outright lie was a great sin, but there was one time when the truth could be stretched. Bragging to the folks at home was far more joy to Apache hunters and warriors than the actual kill. If a man were caught in an outright lie, saying he had killed an enemy or animal when he had not, he was in disgrace and would never be believed again. But if the kill had been made, it was fair for the bragger to stretch the truth as far as he wished. As Gokliya trotted home behind his father, his imagination ran wild, making up the stories he would tell about the brave and daring kill he had made.

From far away Gokliya saw his mother waiting by the wikiup, but again he had to be patient. When he tried to run ahead, his father scowled and pointed back toward his heels; a boy must never run ahead of his father. Besides, there were other rites to be performed before the bragging could begin.

Gokliya's father was very grave when they reached the wikiup. "Wife," he said, "your hunter has returned with his kill. Bring the cloth—the one we saved from my last raid."

Gokliya's mother stooped and went in through the hole that formed the doorway of the wikiup. In a moment she came out again, handing her husband a strip of white cotton cloth. It was about three feet long and a foot wide. Solemnly he passed it between the boy's legs, tying it in place with a thong around the waist, so that a foot of cloth hung down in front and in back. Rising, he stood with his right arm stretched above Gokliya's head, palm down. Lifting his face toward the sky, he spoke in deep and somber tones: "Great Spirit that watches over the deserts and mountains, into Thy keeping we give this hunter of beasts."

This rite marked Gokliya's passing from babyhood into full boyhood. Today he had become a hunter. From this day on he would not go naked but would wear a loincloth, as all Apache men did when on the hunt or the warpath.

The return of a boy from his first successful hunt was a big event in an Apache village. The people gathered quickly, laughing and curious to hear what sort of bragging a boy so young could think up. When they left they were shaking their heads and whispering in wonder and amazement. His own father and mother could hardly believe their eyes and ears.

Few medicine men, and no warrior in the tribe, had such a gift for acting and talking as this seven-year-old grandson of the great Chief Maco. Never before had Gokliya been the center of attention, and his audience stimulated him like strong medicine. Strutting back and forth, crouching, flinging himself flat on the ground, stalking and shooting imaginary arrows, he showed the people what bravery it had taken to make his kill. Sometimes in shouts and sometimes in whispers, words poured from his mouth like water from a bubbling spring. To hear them, one might have believed that the little kangaroo rat was as big and fierce as a grizzly bear.

There seemed to be no end to Gokliya's imagination and his bragging. Sweat dripped from his skinny body and his eyes gleamed wildly as he leaped to safety from the imagined claws of the great rat and shot arrow after arrow into its body. At last his father caught him by the arm and told him, "Enough! No more until you have killed a rabbit or a turkey!"

Though all Apache boys wanted to become hunters and warriors, most of them liked to play. But to Gokliya playing was a waste of time. No game could be so exciting as actual hunting, and no sport so thrilling as the chance to strut and brag of his skills. He would lie motionless for hours, waiting for a rabbit, a rat or a turkey to come within range of his arrows. With each new kill he put on a bragging show, and with each new show he drew more attention to himself. It made him both friends and enemies. The medicine men called him brilliant far beyond his age, but the other boys called him a smarty, a liar and a show-off.

Gokliya cared nothing for what the other boys called him, and he didn't care whether they liked or hated him. He was determined to become the greatest among them, and nothing else mattered. Hour after hour he practiced with his bow and spear, and day after day he hunted alone on the deserts and in the foothills of the mountains. Each month he could shoot his arrows and drive his spears deeper into the trunk of a pine. And each month he ranged farther in his hunt for game.

But the ability to hunt and talk was not the only thing an Apache boy needed if he were someday to become a great chief. He must know the legends of his people, their religion, their rituals and the signs of the heavens. There were, of course, no books, so he must learn from the medicine men. There were no clocks or barometers or compasses, so he must learn to read the stars, moon, the sun, the winds and the clouds. There were no maps, so he must learn to remember every landmark he saw.

When Gokliya was eight years old his training by the medicine men began. They soon discovered that they had a most unusual pupil. The boy was quick to learn and asked so many unexpected questions that they were often at a loss to answer them. Besides, he had an amazing memory. His imagination was so keen that when a story or legend was told him he could picture the action in his mind, and he never forgot it. Anything that he actually saw with his eyes was impressed on his mind so sharply that it remained throughout his lifetime.

At night the stars were the Apaches' clock and compass. Each of the brightest ones was named, and within a few weeks Gokliya could point out and call each one by its Apache name. He learned that the North Star was the one which never moved, and that the Big Dipper turned around it like the hands of a giant clock.

The Apaches had no churches or ministers, but they were very religious. The Great Spirit was called Usen, but there were many other spirits, some good and some bad. The good ones could bring rain, heal the sick, or protect the warriors and hunters from harm. The bad ones could send the lightning, as well as all manner of curses, sickness and death. But these spirits could not be reached except through special rituals which were known only by the medicine men. The rituals were very difficult, but unless they were performed perfectly the spirits would not answer. The training of a boy to become a medicine man usually took many years, but Gokliya's wonderful memory and his ability at acting and mimicry made him a very rapid learner.

Most of Gokliya's training by the medicine men was done in the evenings, and it interfered very little with his hunting. The killing of kangaroo rats, rabbits and turkeys was no longer fun. Month by month he widened the range of his hunting grounds, and his arrow and spearheads sank deeper and deeper into the trunk of his target tree.

Gokliya was no longer a skinny little boy, and though he was not tall for his age, he was stocky and well muscled. Before he was nine he could run twenty-five miles in a day, across scorching deserts and without a drop of water or a bite of food. For many miles around, he knew every foot of the country as well as most boys know their own back yard. He stalked his game with the cunning of the weasel and the patience of the owl, bringing down both foxes and coyotes. But his greatest thrill came when his whistling arrow found the heart of an antelope, the largest and swiftest game on the deserts.

With each new and larger kill Gokliya's bragging grew louder. It annoyed some of the younger warriors, and it increased the hatred of other boys who had little to brag about.

In both mind and body, Gokliya was developed far beyond other Apache boys of his age. The traits that were to mark his whole life were becoming sharp and clear. He cared nothing for the hatred of the other boys, but the applause of the grownups spurred him on to greater efforts. Ambition and determination burned in him like a fire. He would suffer any hardship, brave any danger, and go to any lengths to achieve what he wanted. And he wanted to be the center of attention.

Once he had killed an antelope, Gokliya was no longer satisfied to hunt the game of the deserts. Deer, bear, wildcat and panther were in the high mountains, and glory went to the hunter who brought them home. Gokliya's blood ran hot as he thought of the bragging he would do when he brought home his first panther. But there was more than the bragging or the excitement of the hunt to spur him on. No Apache boy could go into training for the warpath until he had killed a dangerous beast, and Gokliya was beginning to crave the glories of the warpath. He redoubled his practice with his spear and bow.

Gokliya had barely passed his ninth birthday when he could shoot an arrow so swiftly that, from thirty paces, its head would be completely buried in a tree trunk. This was the day for which he had waited so long and practiced so hard. But his father was never to take him to the mountains for his big hunt. Tragedy struck the Apaches and may well have changed the whole course of Gokliya's life.

CHAPTER 5

THE WHITE MAN

AMONG ALL RACES AND PEOPLE THERE ARE GOOD MEN and bad ones. There are men who are just and honorable, and others who are untrustworthy and treacherous. There are men who are generous and men who are greedy. Some will deal fairly with all men, regardless of race or color. Others believe that their own race is superior, that might is right, and that the spoils belong to the victor.

The winter before Gokliya was born the Apaches had their first experience with Americans. These were mountain men, the rough, hardy beaver trappers who pushed our frontier westward across the Rockies. None but the bravest and toughest could live through the raging blizzards of the mountains and the fierce attacks of hostile Indians and wild beasts. To most of the mountain men might was right, Indians were enemies, and beaver skins belonged to anyone who could take them.

When the trappers first came the Apaches looked upon them as neither friends nor enemies. But they were curious about these light-eyed, bearded men who drove their pack mules up the mountain canyons and caught beaver with pieces of iron they hid in the streams. Traps were unknown to the Apaches. From hiding, they watched in amazement as a beaver was caught, pulled under the water and drowned. It was all right with the Apaches if these strange light-eyed men wanted to take a few Apache beaver furs. The white men had lots of things in their camps that the Apaches would like to take in exchange— and did.

The mountain men could not understand this sort of trading. To them the Apaches were sneaking thieves, and if they caught one near their camps or traps, they put a bullet through him.

The younger and hotter-headed warriors wanted to kill the white men in revenge, but Juan José, their old tribal chief, held them back. The "Light Eyes" were doing a better job of catching beaver than the Apaches could; let them alone for the present.

All through the late winter and early spring the Apaches kept a close watch on the trappers, but the Indians were careful to stay out of sight and rifle range. With the first warm days of spring the trappers bound their winter's catch of furs into great bundles and began making ready for their long trip home. This was the day Juan José had been waiting for. He sent swift runners out for fifty miles around, to call the warriors in for a council meeting.

At the tribal council rocks, many miles from the canyon where the trappers were camped, old Juan José sat with his warriors in a circle around him. He had done much thinking during the spring and had kept his thoughts to himself; now he told them to his people.

"It is now four moons that the Light Eyes have been in our mountains. They number no more than my toes and fingers, but they are very smart people. With their traps of iron they have killed many beaver. More than all the Apaches have killed in my lifetime. It is well. They have saved us much labor. These Light Eyes are much braver than the Mexicans. Their knives are long. Their guns shoot far and straight. They think their bullets of lead have made us afraid. They do not know that we too have guns and bullets of lead. This day they gather the furs they would steal from us. At the rising of the sun they think to take them on the long trail to their homeland.

"With one flight of arrows from our hiding places we could kill them all, and no Apaches could be harmed. This cannot be. There may be many more Light Eyes where they came from. They must be told that Apache furs cannot be taken without fair exchange, that Apache lives must be paid for with the lives of light-eyed warriors. They must learn that the Apaches are no cowards, that their warriors are not women. We will not kill them from ambush. At moonrise we will move like shadows into the big canyon, but no warriors will carry gun or bow. At daybreak, we will fight the Light Eyes hand to hand with spear and knives. One white man must die for each Apache they have killed. No more. The rest must be spared to carry word of the Apaches to their people."

As the first dim light of morning filtered into the canyon, the trappers crawled from their blankets, lighted their breakfast fire, and began packing their great bundles of furs onto pack mules. Then, as they ate, they laughed and joked. It had been one of the best winters they'd ever had. Beaver had been plentiful, the furs of excellent quality, and not a man had been killed or injured. "By fire!" one of them hooted. "We sure learnt them thievin' Indians who's boss in these here mountains! Wah! Bet there ain't one of them cowardly varmints come closer'n forty mile since groundhog day."

As if in answer, the Apache war whoop filled the canyon like the howl of a thousand wolves. From behind every boulder and tree leaped a red-brown shrieking Apache, naked except for his loincloth. With spears high and knives flashing they circled the little camp in a screeching, writhing dance of death.

Any but American mountain men would have been thrown into a wild panic, but these men had faced sudden death a hundred times before. Experience had taught them that, when fighting Indians, a lightning-fast attack was the best defense. Most Indians would run when blood began to flow.

There was no time for priming flintlock rifles or pistols, not even time to reach for them. Yanking their long hunting knives from their belts as they leaped to their feet, the trappers charged into the howling circle of Apaches.

But these Indians were a new breed to the mountain men; they didn't run, but fought back like enraged wildcats. The battle was as short as it was fierce. In less than two minutes nearly half of the trappers and two Apaches lay dying. Then the voice of Juan José rose above the clamor, "Enju!" (It is well!) The Apache warriors fell back, and the few trappers who were not mortally wounded raced for their lives down the canyon.

To the Apaches the score was now even. There was no reason for either side to hate the other. The Light Eyes had killed a few Apaches while trying to steal the beaver furs; the Apaches had killed a few white men to get back the furs. The Light Eyes had lived on Apache deer and elk for four moons; the Apaches had taken a few pack mules and some camp equipment in exchange.

That summer other Americans came into the Apache homeland. They were good men, and the Apaches showed no hostility toward them. One came with mules loaded with beads, trinkets, pots, pans and bright-colored cloth. These he traded for deer, panther and wildcat skins. Kit Carson, then a boy of nineteen, hunted among them and made a lifelong friend of Mangas Coloradas, the giant subchief of Juan José's tribe.

As the years passed more white men came. A few of them were traders with trinkets and bright cloth. Several bands of mountain men came into the northern part of the Apache homeland. Ewing Young, with Kit Carson and a band of twenty men, trapped the headwaters of the Gila River. Once in a while there was a skirmish. A few Apache warriors and a few mountain men were killed, but that was to be expected in a wild country. There was no hatred between the Americans and the Apaches.

The spring that Gokliya shot his first antelope another white trader came into the Apache homeland. His name was Johnson, and he made his camp near the tribal council rocks. Johnson didn't bring trinkets and bright cloth for trading with the Apaches. He wasn't interested in the few dollars that could be made by honest trading for deer and panther skins. He had come to get rich quick, and he knew the weakness of all Indians for firewater. His mules were loaded with casks of cheap American whiskey.

The Apaches had never tasted whiskey but, like all

other Indians, quickly learned that a little of it would make them feel frisky and happy.

Johnson was generous with his firewater until he had made good friends of Old Chief Juan José and many of the young Apache warriors. Then he got down to business. The old chief could have firewater whenever he wanted it, but the others must bring a horse or mule to trade for each cupful.

The Apaches had no mules and few horses, but their enemies, the Mexicans, had plenty—and the Apaches had become experts at stealing them. As soon as Johnson set the price on his whiskey the Apaches went wild in their raids on Mexican ranches. No day passed without a band of Apache raiders slipping southward across the deserts. Each night dozens of stolen horses and mules were driven northward to Johnson's camp.

Johnson had known what would happen when he set the price on his whiskey, and had planned for it in advance. Before coming to the Apache homeland he had made a deal with a band of Mexican outlaws. They would pay him ten dollars for each stolen animal, then sell it back to a Mexican rancher at a big profit.

The Apache raids on the Mexicans became unbearable. Driven by their craving for whiskey, the warriors became more daring and ruthless than ever before. Many ranchers, villagers and cavalrymen were ambushed and killed when they tried to fight off swarms of raiders. In desperation, the Mexican government released hundreds of convicts from prisons, moved them to the frontier, and increased the bounties on Apache scalps.

Johnson was getting rich fast, but not fast enough. He took a trip to Mexico and made another deal. This time it was not with outlaws but with officials of the government.

When Johnson returned he went straight to see his friend Chief Juan José. The old chief was glad to see his white friend. They had a fine visit, and the jug passed freely.

"This here's the last drop out'n the last barrel." Johnson laughed as he passed the jug. "I'm on my way up to Santa Fe to fetch another forty barrels. Tell you want I'll do, Chief. I been aimin' to do somethin' real nice for you and your folks. I'll fetch back a heap of grub and pretties for the women folks, and we'll put on the all-firedest feast this here country ever seen."

Juan José waited anxiously for his friend's return from Santa Fe. When runners brought word that Johnson was coming with a long, heavily loaded pack train and several other white men, the old chief was delighted. His friend was going to keep his word. The mules must be loaded with food and presents for the great feast, and the other white men must be coming to help Johnson with the preparations. Runners were hurried off to invite all the Apaches within a hundred miles to come in to the great feast.

Many of the warriors were away on raids or hunts, but hundreds of those who weren't, together with their women and children, hurried to the tribal council rocks.

Johnson and his helpers had made great preparations. Pits had been dug, fires built in them, and whole beefs were roasting. Sacks of corn meal, sugar and beans were piled high in front of a clump of bushes. On top of the sacks were laid out strings of beads, bright pieces of cloth, shiny tin pans and trinkets of all kinds. When the jug had been passed freely, Johnson shouted from behind the pile of food sacks for people to come and get their presents. Everyone could have a pretty present and all the food he or she could carry away.

The Apaches crowded forward, anxious to have first choice of the presents. Nearly a thousand of them were packed into a pushing, squeezing mob. Suddenly Johnson touched the lighted end of his cigar to the fuse of a cannon that he had hidden among the food sacks. The cannon was loaded to the muzzle with rusty nails, pieces of broken chain and scraps of iron.

It is said that five hundred Apaches were killed in this massacre. The cannon fire missed old Chief Juan José, but Johnson took care of that; he shot him from behind with a pistol.

The Apaches who had not been killed or mortally wounded ran, panic-stricken, for cover. In fear of this terrible, unknown engine of death they fled far out into the deserts and mountains. Before Mangas Coloradas, the new tribal chief, could gather his warriors, Johnson had escaped to Mexico. With him he carried the hundreds of Apache scalps he had promised to deliver to the officials.

CHAPTER 6

CHIEF MANGAS
COLORADAS

GOKLIYA AND HIS MOTHER HAD ESCAPED THE Johnson Massacre. Neither of them had received so much as a scratch on the body. But they had received a deep wound of their minds—an undying hatred for every white man. This wound would cost more American lives than all the Apache scalps Johnson had sold to the Mexicans.

Gokliya and his mother were not alone in their grief and anger. Hatred for the Americans flared to a white heat among all the people of the tribe. As the fiercest warriors returned from their hunting and raiding, they gathered into war parties. They knew nothing of the country to the north and east, but it was from there that the white men had come. Where these had come from there must be more. Wherever they were, the Apache warriors were determined to hunt them down and kill every one of them in revenge.

Mangas Coloradas, the new tribal chief, was a giant in both size and wisdom. He sent runners to hunt out every living warrior of the tribe. On the fourth sunrise, they were to come to a great war council at a new meeting place at the warm springs. In the meantime, they must stay off the warpath and go on no hunts or raids.

In the three days it took to gather the warriors, Mangas Coloradas neither slept nor ate. Hidden away in a lonely canyon, he sat with his great head hunched nearly to his knees, thinking. His people were in deep trouble. To the south of their homeland were the Mexicans, offering enormous bounties for Apache scalps. To the west were the unfriendly Papagos and Maricopas, greedy for Mexican bounties. And now, from the north and east came these white men with guns that could kill five hundred people at a single blast.

Worse still, the fighting strength of the tribe had been greatly weakened by the massacre. Mangas Coloradas himself was a new and untried chief who had not yet won the confidence of his people. His warriors were thirsting for revenge and American blood. He could make himself a great hero by leading them on the warpath. But would they listen to him? Would they keep him for their chief if he refused to let them go on the warpath against theAmericans?

As the first rays of the fourth sunrise glinted on the warm springs near the Rio Grande, they reddened the sullen, angry faces of the greatest Apache war council that had ever gathered. The warriors had been coming in throughout the night. Since the fading of the morning star, they had sat cross-legged and brooding, waiting for the arrival of their new and untried chief. Grunts and angry murmurs were passing between the older warriors when a lone figure walked slowly from a nearby canyon.

Looking neither right nor left, Mangas Coloradas moved in measured, unhurried steps toward the deep circle of angry warriors. His massive head was bowed. His bull-like shoulders and body were wrapped in an old red blanket. Here was no fierce war chief, frantic to lead his fighting men against the hated whites. Whispers buzzed back and forth between the band leaders and older warriors at the center of the circle. Far back, at its outside edge, the young, hot-blooded warriors grunted, shrugged their shoulders and grimaced mockingly.

As the new chief neared the seated warriors the murmuring and grimacing stopped. In silence, young and old moved aside, opening a pathway to the little mound at the center of the meeting grounds. So deep in thought that he walked like a man in his sleep, Mangas Coloradas passed between the sullen, scowling rows of warriors. As he reached the mound he let the blanket drop from his shoulders. Raising one arm, he turned silently and slowly, studying the faces of his warriors, his great body towering six and a half feet on widely saddle-bowed legs. Solemnly his deep voice boomed out across the stillness.

"My brothers, the Great Spirit has hidden His face from His people. The evil spirits frown upon us. The voices of our medicine men are not heard above the clouds that hang over us. Their rituals are not seen. The faces of the good spirits are turned from us. They smile upon our enemies."

Turning slowly, Mangas Coloradas raised his voice until it rang like a great bell. "Why is this, my brothers? I will tell you! It is because, for many moons, we have turned our own faces away from the good spirits. We have tasted the strong red medicine that our enemy, the Mexican, keeps in bottles of glass. We have burned our tongues and our brains with the stronger medicine that the white men have brought among us in little barrels.

"From where the sun rises to where he sets, from where the unmoving star lives in the northern sky to where the great cross of stars shines in the south, Usen has made the world and given it to His people. To feed us He has made the deer, the elk and the antelope. To clothe us He has made the bear, the panther and the beaver. From beyond the sun and the stars He has sent strangers to bring His people the horse and the cow.

Until we tasted the strong medicine of these strangers we were strong. With our strength and our skill we took what we needed of the things Usen had made for us, and of what He had sent to us from beyond the sun and stars. Then we tasted the strong medicine of the Mexicans, and they set bounties on our scalps.

"Now we have tasted the stronger medicine of the white man. It has made us fools! When it is hot in our bellies we are brave; we forget our need for the good spirits. We will not listen to our own medicine men. We take many more horses and mules than we need. We trade them for more of the white man's strong medicine. Again we are brave until we go to sleep. When we wake we are sick, sniveling babies. We listened to the words of a white man as if he were a great spirit. We crowded like cows to carrion, begging for food and trinkets from his hand. It was not food and trinkets that he gave. It was death and grief.

"Are we fools? The strong medicine of the white man is still in our blood. Our eyes are still red from weeping for our wives and children. We have seen the white man's great gun kill them as the blizzard kills the flowers on the mountain. Many of our warriors have gone to the hunting ground in the sky. Our arm is weak on the bow. The good spirits have turned their faces from us. Yet many of you would take the warpath against the white man. You would follow his trail into the unknown land he comes from. You would shoot your arrows into the wikiups where his great guns are hidden. Are we fools?"

The faces of the warriors were no longer sullen and angry. Many hung their heads in shame. From here and there came cries of, "No!" "No!"

An old headman rose unsteadily from his place. His face was deeply wrinkled, his tongue burned many times by Johnson's whiskey. His sharp voice lifted above the cries of the others, "We hear your words, Mangas Coloradas. They are words of wisdom. We have been fools, but are no longer. Speak on, that your people may share the wisdom of their chief."

Shouts of, *"Enju!" "Enju!"* (It is well! It is well!) rose from a hundred throats.

Mangas knew he had won the confidence of his people. Now he must lead them with all the wisdom and skill at his command. His words no longer whipped like a lash, and his voice no longer pealed out with the angry tones of a great bell. Anxiously the warriors leaned forward to listen.

"Does the brave warrior take his gun and bow and go forth to fight the blizzard? No, my brothers! Does he go on the long raid when the winds and the signs of the sky say another blizzard may come? Does he leave his wife and his children to starve and freeze? No, my brothers! He hunts the deer in the nearby foothills. He gathers new brush to make his wikiup strong and warm.

"Does a wise man hate the snow because one blizzard blew down his wikiup and killed some of his children? No, my brothers! He builds a stronger wikiup, his wife bears him more children, and he welcomes the gentle snow that will make the desert green.

"Four suns ago a blizzard struck from the north. It blew down the wikiup that was our tribe. It killed our chief and many of our people. With the faces of the good spirits turned from us, another blizzard may be coming from beyond the northern mountains. We will not run out like fools to fight against it. We will not go on the long warpath. We will stay at home to rebuild and strengthen the wikiup that is our tribe. We will turn our faces to our own medicine men, to the good spirits of our fathers before us. We will never again taste the strong medicine of the white man and the Mexican.

"This day you will go back to your villages. On the rising of the fourth sun you will return. You will bring with you every boy above the age of ten. These are the branches we will gather to strengthen our wikiup. These we will train to guard the homeland Usen has given us, to hold it from those who would try to take it from us."

Again Mangas Coloradas turned slowly, studying the faces of his warriors. "Who speaks for a people?" he demanded.

"Their chief! Their chief!" came the answer.

"Then hear me!" Mangas shouted. "Is it not the chief

of the Mexicans who offers bounties for Apache scalps?"

"*Ayee! Ayee!*" The answer came from many throats.

"Then, as long as the bounties stand we kill any Mexican that our sun and our stars shine upon."

"*Ayee! Ayee! Enju!*"

"Was it the chief of the white men who brought the evil medicine among us? No! Was there a chief among those who brought the great gun that killed when our people reached out their hands for food? No! Did their chief send them to do this? I do not know. But this I do know: when the fathers are bad, all the children are bad."

Mangas Coloradas' glance swept across the upturned faces around him. "All the children of a good father may not be good. Our great chief Juan José was a good father, but among you I see men who speak with a double tongue, men who would kill a brother if they dared. I have known good white men and bad. Both have been among us. We do not hate the white snow because it sometimes rides on the treacherous blast of a blizzard. We cannot hate all the white men because some of them are treacherous. They are clever people. They know many things the Apaches do not know. We will learn from them. Those who are honest we will treat with honor. Those who would rob and kill us we will treat with robbery and death. Go, my brothers! I have spoken!"

CHAPTER 7

THE SEEDS OF HATE

THE HEADMAN OF THE VILLAGE WHERE GOKLIYA lived was old; his sight was dimming, but his mind and memory were as clear as a mountain stream. When he returned from the great war council he repeated to his people every word the new chief had spoken.

Gokliya listened in wonder and amazement. Never before had he heard such oratory—words spoken with such power and eloquence. Not a sound or gesture escaped him, but it was the rolling sound of the words rather than their meaning that held him spellbound. He was only annoyed because Mangas Coloradas had called for boys above the age of ten instead of nine.

Beside him his mother snuffed and grunted. As the headman neared the end of his recital, her face turned crimson with rage. Snatching Gokliya by an arm, she yanked him out of the crowd around the speaker. "Do not listen! It is lies! Lies!" she hissed as she hurried him toward their wikiup.

Gokliya had never seen his mother so furious, but the music of Mangas Coloradas' word still rang in his ears. As he hurried along with his mother, phrase after phrase ran through his mind. He forced his voice deep into his throat, to make the words roll as much as he could, and shouted, "Go, my brothers! I have spoken!"

Apaches were almost never rough with their children, but at this moment, Gokliya's mother clapped her hand hard across his mouth. When they reached their wikiup she fairly flung him through the entrance. Following him in, she grabbed him by both arms, held him before her, and glared into his eyes. "Lies! Lies!" she screamed. "Lies for fools and babies! Wipe them from your memory! Forget your ears have ever heard them!"

But is not Mangas Coloradas our great chief?" Gokliya asked. "His words are . . ."

"Great chief, bah!! Coyote chief! She sneered. "His words are the howling of a cowardly coyote, afraid to fight when the wolf has killed its young. Great chief! We were better to have an old woman for a chief! Will not the she-bear fight when the wolf pack sweeps down upon her cubs?"

The giant Mangas Coloradas had been Gokliya's hero since he could first remember. Now he tried to defend him against his mother's anger. "Mangas Coloradas is a brave warrior," he told her. "Did he not fight a whole village of Mexicans single-handed?"

"Mexicans! More coyotes!" she scoffed. "One day, my son, you will be a great chief. But I would rather I had buried you beside your father than to see you be a coyote chief, a chief who dares only fight other coyotes. You will be the wolf of the Apache warpath. You will fight this white wolf pack that comes down from the north to kill your people and steal their homeland—you will *kill, kill, kill!*

Gokliya pulled away from his mother's grasp, squared his shoulders and boasted, "I can kill now! What boy above ten years old has killed more antelope than I? And have I not killed the fox and the coyote? Why did Mangas Coloradas not say boys above nine instead of ten? I can run farther and faster than any boy in our band. When the older boys hide in fear from the lightning, I am not afraid. I can shoot straighter and harder than any of them. My spear is swifter. What older boy can bury his arrowheads in the heart of a pine tree? I could kill more enemies than all of them put together."

Gokliya's mother had smiled as he began his boasting, but as he went on her look changed to pride and determination. "For many summers you will be too young to kill enemies, my son, but your feet are already strong enough to tread the first steps of the warpath. At the rising of the sun you shall go with the warriors and older boys. I shall give my word that you are above the age of ten."

Gokliya wanted to go with the warriors more than he had ever wanted anything in his life, but he could hardly believe his ears. The only punishments his mother had ever given him had been for telling lies. She had told him it was the worst sin an Apache could commit. And now she was going to give her word to an outright lie. He looked at her in unbelieving amazement.

She knew what he was thinking and answered before he could speak. "When the great fire sweeps across the dry grasslands, is it a sin to set other fires in its pathway, to stop it and save the wikiup? When our chief lies to his people, telling them there are good white men who are their friends, is it a sin to lie to that chief about one year of a boy's age? No, my son! It is only a little fire that may help to stop the great blaze that is sweeping down upon us from the north.

"Antelope killing is for boys who hide from the lightning," she went on. "The warpath against the Mexicans is for the brave and the strong. But courage and strength alone are as broken arrows against the white men.

Their tongues are forked and nimble, they are as sly as the weasel, as scheming as the fox and as deadly as the rattlesnake. One white man smiles into a red man's face and calls him his friend while another plunges a knife into his back. Their smiles and their double tongues are more to be feared than their great gun that speaks with a thousand deaths.

"How many of our people could the great gun have killed if Juan José had not been fooled by the white man's smile and his words? How many would still be alive if Juan José had not called us together to take the food from the white man's hand? And now they have smiled in the face of our new chief. Their cunning words have turned his stupid head. Now, while the buzzards still fly over the graves of our dead, he tells us there are good white men, that they are our friends. Bah! Such a chief can lead us nowhere but to the grave.

"Your mother is only a woman. She can never go on the warpath. She can never be a chief. But if her son listens to her words and carries them always in his heart, she will have reared a chief who will drive the white men from the earth. Your brain is quick and cunning, your tongue is nimble, and the blood of fighting chiefs runs in your veins. It is time your feet were on the warpath.

"At the rising of the sun you will go. From our warriors you will learn to fight with the gun, the spear and the bow. From the white man you will learn to fight with the smile and the double tongue. As the great fire must be fought with fire, so the white man's treachery must be fought with treachery. Sleep now; the path you take is a long one! Your mother goes to give her word that you are above the age of ten."

As Gokliya's mother left the wikiup, the boy wrapped himself in his deerskin and lay down. But the words he had just heard went through his mind many times before he slept. When he woke, pale light showed at the entrance of the wikiup. Against it, he saw the dark form of his mother, sitting motionless. As he stirred, she tossed twigs on the embers of the fire and hung a pot of venison to heat. A flame sprang up, and in its light he saw that she had not slept. The fine red blanket his father had worn to council meetings was folded and lying beside her. On it were laid his war spear, bow and quiver of arrows.

As Gokliya ate, his mother sat in silence. When he had finished she spoke solemnly. "The trail you take is long. Your father can speak no words of caution to his son; his voice is forever still. Hear then the words of your mother: If our coyote chief talks more of treating the white men with honor, do not listen. Close your ears and let them hear again the scream of the dying. Close your eyes and let them see only the graves of your father and your people.

"Never forget that all white men are treacherous. Take no food from their hands; they bait traps for wild beasts

51

with food. You have seen them bait their trap for your people with food. Go, my son! Carry in your hands the weapons of your father, and in your heart the words of your mother." Having spoken, she turned her back toward him and sat in silence as the boy gathered up his war gear and started away on the long trail.

CHAPTER 8

FIRST STEPS OF THE LONG TRAIL

GOKLIYA WAS THE YOUNGEST OF ALL THE APACHE BOYS brought in for training. The oldest and largest boys were sent into the mountains with the hunters. Only those who proved their bravery against wild beasts would be trained as warriors.

The boys in their early teens were put in the scout camps. Their trainers were the warriors most highly skilled in scouting enemy country without being caught, in following almost invisible trails, and in running great distances to carry messages. Before a boy could graduate and join the hunters he must know every landmark of his homeland, and have run fifty miles a day without food or water. Nor was that all. He must be able to sneak in and out of camps without being caught, and to follow a trail that was at least a week old.

The youngest boys, Gokliya among them, were put to tending the horse herds. Tending an Apache horse herd was no child's play but rough, hard training. An Apache warrior could outrun any horse across wide, dry deserts or up steep mountains. But in warfare a horse's quick bursts of speed and ability to carry heavy loads were as necessary as arrows and bullets. Only war horses were prized by the Apaches. And since they raised none, each must be stolen, guarded from enemy raids, and trained for the Apache's own type of warfare. Only the toughest and swiftest horses were trained, and these must be taught to be handled without the use of reins. An Apache warrior needed both hands free for bow or gun.

The warriors in charge of the horse boys were the ones who had proved themselves to be the most clever at stealing horses, training them for war, hiding them from enemies, and torturing them into running at top speed until they dropped in their tracks. The plains Indians had love for their horses, but the Apaches had none. They believed that their Great Spirit, Usen, had made the horse only to serve them in war and to feed them.

Apache boys, like all other boys, were fond of games, and the warriors in the horse camps made games out of the boys' training. The horse boys were divided into bands of six or eight, each with a warrior trainer and a herd of a dozen or so horses. Then the bands competed in games against one another. This was done even before the boys were allowed to ride. They learned to herd their horses afoot, to trail down and gather a scattered herd, to scatter the herd of another band, to steal horses from it, and to hide them away where the other bands could not find them.

Next, the boys were taught to catch a horse, to mount it, and to ride. All the Apache horses had been stolen from the Mexicans, and most of them were wild, unbroken broncos. No lassos were used for catching these broncos, and no saddles or bridles were used for riding them. A boy must learn to work his way up to a bronco without frightening it, to talk gently to it and soothe it until he could grasp its mane. Then he must fling himself high on its neck, throw a leg over its back, and cling with his hands and knees as it pitched and bucked. When the boy was older, he would learn to catch a running horse by stunning it with a blunt stone-tipped arrow shot against the head.

By the time Gokliya had been in the horse camps a year he was the pride of his trainer, and was made leader of his band. He could ride as well as many of the warriors, and seemed to be afraid of nothing. The other boys shied away from horses that struck, kicked and slashed with their teeth, but these were the ones Gokliya liked best.

Already the urge to fight and to have his own way was in him, and he had contempt for any horse without the same spirit. Time and again he was knocked down, kicked or raked with flashing teeth, but it only made his fighting blood run hotter. No hurt was great enough to stop him. Picking himself up, he would tackle the bronco again. When at last he was able to fling himself onto its back, he matched its viciousness with his own. Whipping and gouging, he would run the bronco till it accepted him as its master.

Though avoiding the roughest horses, all the boys were riding by the time Gokliya was made leader of his band. Now they began to learn a new game. This was the game of warfare—the ambush, the lightning attack, and the ruthless race to escape a stronger enemy.

No longer did the boys steal horses from the other bands by stealth and cunning. Each boy carried his bow, a quiver of blunt-tipped reed arrows, and longer reeds for spears. When least expected, one band would ride cautiously to surround the sleeping camp of another. Suddenly, the Apache war whoop would rip the stillness, and the raiders would charge the camp in a racing, driving attack.

Springing from their deerskins with bow in hand, the defenders would try to break up the raid and save their horse herd. Or, if their lookouts had spied the approaching enemy, the defenders would set an ambush. The battles were often swift and fierce, but the boys were seldom badly hurt. The reed arrows and spears broke when they struck, but each had been dipped in Indian paint, so that it would leave a red mark wherever it hit. If a boy's horse was hit it was considered dead. He must jump to the ground and fight afoot unless he could catch and mount another horse. If a boy himself was hit he was out of the battle.

Gokliya proved to be an exceedingly smart leader. He drove the boys in his band just as hard as he drove himself and the horses he rode. Though youngest of all the herd boys, he was one of the strongest and quickest. He could fight wickedly, and was ruthless in his punishment of any boy in his band who showed fear or carelessness.

He always pretended that his raids were being made against a camp of the hated white men. There were times when the tricks he used were close to treachery. He would grease his body heavily before a raid, so that the paint mark from a spear or arrow would not stain his skin and could be wiped away. All the boys of his band might be hit and supposedly killed, but no one could prove that Gokliya had ever been touched. Few camps could withstand the fierceness of his raids, and the horse herd of his band soon became the largest.

With its growing horse herd, Gokliya's band became the target of all the other bands. But he was as clever in defending it as he was in his raiding. Very soon after becoming a herd boy he had noticed that burros were tattletales. If there was one in a herd of horses, it was sure to bray long before a rider came within sight. Once in a while there was a burro in a stolen horse herd brought back from Mexico by the warriors. And each time, Gokliya was careful to steal it and put it into the herd of his own band. With half a dozen tattletales among his horses, it was easy for him to have an ambush set up whenever another band came raiding—and he became an artist at ambushing.

Gokliya was twelve when he graduated from horse herding and went to join the scouts. By that time there was no other boy in the tribe who was so skillful at raiding, so clever at horse stealing, or so cunning at setting an ambush. His teachers were sorry to see him go, but the other boys were not. Those in his own band distrusted and feared him; those in the other bands hated him for being a cheat and a braggart.

In the horse camps there had been time for the boys to rest and play. After the first year most of their work had been done on horseback, and there had been little need for great endurance. In the scout camps it was quite different. A horse might give a scout away in enemy country, and it could not be hidden quickly in times of emergency. A scout must do his work afoot, and his endurance must be built up far beyond that of a horse.

At first the boys' only training was in building up their resistance to fatigue, hunger, thirst, heat and cold. They were given no rest from dawn to dark. Day after day the distances they were made to run, crawl on hands and knees, or wriggle on their bellies were increased. On the hottest days their training was done in the broiling deserts; on the coldest, in the snows of the mountains. They were taught to live off the land. Their only food was mesquite beans, grass seeds or berries they could find on their way. Often a whole day was passed without a drop of water.

Most of the boys complained and grumbled about the hardships of their training. Some of the weaker ones played out, got sick and had to be sent home. Others shirked whenever they could, and the warriors who were their trainers had to drive them. Right from the first Gokliya thrived on the hard life. He did no grumbling and needed no driving. The training his father had given him as a little boy stood him in good stead, and his determination not to be outdone drove him to suffer any hardship without complaining. His body and legs grew lean and tough, his shoulders broadened as his lungs expanded from continual running. He pushed to the front among the scouts as rapidly as he had among the herd boys. Before the end of his first year his trainer appointed him leader of his band.

When the actual scouting was begun Gokliya was outstanding. His eye was sharp, his mind quick to learn, and his memory almost unbelievable. There was no hardship too severe to be endured, no mountain too steep to be climbed, and no trail too long or dim to be followed.

By the end of his second year, Gokliya was by far the best scout of any boy in training. With his knowledge of the stars and his wonderful memory for landmarks, he could find his way back over any path he had ever trod. He could follow a track so faint that no other boy could even find it. Every dislodged pebble, every broken twig, and even the dew on the grass was a sign he could read. He could sneak into the camp of another band as noiselessly as moonlight, leave a token of his having been there, then get away as soundless as he had come.

The third year of scout training was the most severe. Each scouting band was left in charge of its leader, and each was in competition with all the others. Trainers would run ahead, sometimes for two or three hundred miles, into the wildest and roughest Mexican mountains. After their trails were two or three days old the bands of boys were sent out to pick up and follow the trail of a rival trainer. There was glory for the band that could unravel the track and run down the trainer, but disgrace for any band that lost the trail completely.

Time after time Gokliya's band won the glory, and other bands were disgraced. Gokliya was successful not only because of his skill as a tracker but also because of his ruthlessness and cunning. He was determined that he and his band should have the glory, and would go to any lengths to gain it.

A trainer always left a roundabout and intricate trail for the boys to unravel, but Gokliya would seldom follow it. With his wonderful memory he would know that sooner or later the trail must cross a certain mountain pass, maybe fifty miles ahead, and he would drive his band straight for it. Though he drove his band unsparingly, he drove himself even harder, making long runs to hunt out the trails of other trainers, cover them, and leave false trails to confuse and mislead rival bands. If his own boys trailed and lagged he bullied and whipped them on to the very limit of their endurance. When, at fifteen, he was moved to the hunters' camp, his boys were glad to see him go.

CHAPTER 9

THE WAYS OF
THE WARPATH

THE HUNTERS' CAMPS WERE SCATTERED WIDELY AMONG the highest mountains in the Apache homeland and were seldom kept more than a few days in the same place. In each camp a band of boys in their late teens were being trained for the warpath. Here, for the first time, they learned to handle firearms and were taught the tricks of using knife and spear in hand-to-hand battles. Whenever they were not hunting deer, elk, bear or panther they were at war with the boys from other camps.

Firearms were never used in this warfare. But although the spear and arrows had no stone tips, and the knives were of soft wood, the battles were fierce and wounds were many and painful. Prisoners were the prize of this warfare. When a boy was taken prisoner he became a slave of his captors until he could escape or was recaptured by his own band.

The constant moving of the camps and the fact that the bands were not all of the same strength made scouting very important. Gokliya was the youngest boy in any of the hunter camps, but he soon proved himself to be the most cunning scout. It was often thirty or forty miles from one camp to another. Each was pitched where it could best be defended, and lookouts were on guard constantly. None of these things bothered Gokliya. During his three years in the scouts he had been over every mountain chain in the Apache homeland. Filed away in his never-failing memory were pictures of every canyon, mountain, and the territory beyond.

Many of the scouts hunted enemy camps as a dog hunts a covey of birds—searching back and forth through the mountains until a fresh sign was found. But not Gokliya. Just as he had been able to foretell which mountain pass a trainer of scouts would cross, so could he foretell the most likely places for an enemy band to pitch its camp. This was no second sight, but careful thinking and planning. As he ran through the night toward a mountain chain where he believed an enemy band to be camped, his mind was as busy as his legs. He reasoned where he would pitch his camp if he were leader of that band, where he would place his lookouts, and where he would hold his prisoners.

Striking straight for the most likely campsite, he would creep up to it in the first dim light of morning, avoiding any spot where he himself would have placed a lookout. If the camp were not where he expected to find it, he would move on in the same way to the next most likely place.

Once any enemy camp was discovered, Gokliya did not race back, as most of the other boys did, to carry the word to his own band. There was much to be learned before a successful attack could be made. He must find out the strength of the enemy, where each of its lookouts were kept posted, the best angle from which to make a surprise attack, the best route of escape if overpowered, and the probability of the camp's being moved.

If the strength of the enemy was clearly too great for his own band he wasted no time there, but moved on to discover a weaker enemy. If signs showed the camp to be several days old and apt to be moved, he carefully scouted each new location where it might be pitched. When he returned to his own camp he would lay out the whole plan of battle for his band leader. His plans were always good, but no band leader wanted the youngest boy in camp telling him how he should plan his attack.

It took courage for a boy to go into battle, even though the enemy was armed only with wooden knives and blunt-pointed spears and arrows; but Gokliya's courage was equal to his cunning. As in the horse camps, he pretended that each attack was being made against a camp of white men. On the way into battle he worked himself into a frenzy, repeating in his mind the words of his mother, and imagining that he heard again the screams of the dying in the Johnson massacre. At hand-to-hand fighting no boy of any age could stand up against the fierceness, speed and cleverness of his attack. Feinting, dodging and slashing, he whipped his knife in and out like flashes of lightning. His excitement in battle seemed uncontrollable. Often he ripped and wounded his supposed enemy even after the other boy had cried, "Surrender!"

Gokliya never became so skillful with firearms as some of the other boys, but his bow arm was stronger than that of any other. His arrow flew swifter and straighter, and his hunting spear was deadly at a hundred feet. By the time he was sixteen he had brought down dozens of deer and elk, he had run a panther until it took to a tree, then shot it down with bow and arrow. He had killed bear with both gun and bow. He was now determined to prove himself with spear and knife alone.

No Apache boy could go on a raid with the warriors until he had proved his courage in a hand-to-hand fight with a full-grown bear or other fierce animal. None could fight an actual enemy of the tribe until he had proved his endurance and bravery on four raids, and had been admitted to the council of warriors.

Almost always it was a band leader who went out for a hand-to-hand fight with a fierce beast, but Gokliya had never become a band leader in the hunters' camps. There the boys chose their own leaders. Though Gokliya was the best scout among them and had captured the most prisoners and killed the most bears, he was never chosen. It angered him, made him vicious with the other boys, and more determined than ever that he should be first to be admitted to the council of warriors.

Gokliya's chance came unexpectedly. One crisp fall day the band to which Gokliya belonged was returning to camp from a long hunt. As often happened, Gokliya was well in the lead of the other boys. At the end of the line came the warriors who were the boys' teachers. Suddenly, as Gokliya rounded a mountain spur, he heard an angry, snarling hiss. There, crouched in a notch among the rocks, was a great male panther. It sprang before he could whip an arrow from his quiver and string it to his bow.

A panther will seldom attack a man unless cornered, but when he does attack he is the most dangerous of any animal on our continent. Any boy without as quick a mind and body as Gokliya's would have been killed instantly. His hunting spear was in his right hand. In a lightning-fast sweep his left yanked the knife from his loincloth. Crouching to avoid the striking, ripping claws, he lunged his spear at the panther's throat. It struck fair, but was jerked from his hand and broken like a dry twig. As the great body flashed above his head he slashed at the belly with his knife.

Blood covered the knife, but the wounds were not deep and only served to make the panther more furious. Thrown off balance, it landed in a heap, rolled to its feet and sprang again. Gokliya went down with the panther on top of him. Quick as the great cat itself, he rolled and slashed with his knife. Over and over, round and round they went—the panther ripping with claws and teeth. Gokliya's knife flashing like the fangs of a rattlesnake.

The warriors watched with lifted guns, afraid to shoot for fear of hitting Gokliya. The boys stood spellbound, awed by the writhing, twisting fury of the fight. Blood covered the rolling, thrashing boy and beast.

It was soon over. No fight so furious could last more than a minute or two. Gokliya's knife found an artery, blood spurted high, and the panther's strength went with it. As the warriors rushed in to pull Gokliya away, the great beast stretched out and lay twitching in its death struggle.

Gokliya was scratched and mauled, blood flowed from a dozen rips in his flesh, but his pride and determination kept him on his feet. Now he had proved himself best of all the boys in training, even though they had never chosen him for their leader. Now the warriors would have to let him go with them on raids.

Two moons had come to their full before Gokliya's wounds were healed. Deep red scars still covered his body when he took his first long raiding trail behind the warriors.

An Apache boy was almost a slave on his four proving trips with the warriors. He could speak not a word, let no water touch his lips, and eat only the food that was left over after the warriors had eaten. They would cover forty or fifty miles afoot in a day, but he had to cover nearly twice that number, hunting far from the trail and bringing in enough meat to keep them in food. He must obey every order given him, carry whatever load was put upon him, and face any danger that arose. Even if attacked, he could not fight against an enemy, but must make his escape as best he could. If he spoke, showed fear or tiredness, or if he failed to bring in enough meat, he would not be admitted to the council of warriors. One voice raised against him for any failure would be enough to keep him out.

Gokliya passed his seventeenth birthday just before he completed his fourth raiding trip, and was the youngest boy to come before the council for approval as a warrior. All the warriors of the tribe sat in council to judge a boy's fitness to become a member and a warrior of the tribe. He must tell of his deeds that made him worthy, but this was no time for wild bragging or stretching the truth. One challenge of his word, his bravery, his endurance or his fitness would disqualify him.

Gokliya stood at the center of the council meeting with his head held high. Was he not grandson of a great chief? Would he not one day be a great chief himself? His pride would not let him stand pleadingly before this council of warriors. He was careful to tell no lies, but his recital of his deeds was close to bragging. He had been the best rider, the best raider and the best ambusher in the horse boys' camp. He had tracked down and overtaken more trainers than any other scout in the camps. He was the best scout and the best fighter in the hunters' camps; he had killed more deer, elk and bear than any other boy. He was the only Apache boy who had killed a panther in a hand-to-hand fight. On raiding trips into Mexico he had escaped from the enemy when warriors with him had been killed or captured.

Around Gokliya the warriors sat with scowls on their faces. The deeds he claimed were greater than those of any of their own sons—greater than many of them could have claimed for themselves. Their faces showed that they did not like this haughty boy with his high head and grand claims. They glanced back and forth among themselves, looking for someone who might rise and challenge this boy. Would there be one to tell of some time when Gokliya had shown cowardice, when he had become exhausted on the trail, or that he had lied in making some of his claims?

But no one spoke. The council sat silent and glum for

several minutes. At last Mangas Coloradas rose, stepped forward and placed the warrior's band on Gokliya's head. Raising his arm, he spoke the words that would make Gokliya a member of the council and a warrior of the tribe.

CHAPTER 10

ALOPE

BECOMING A WARRIOR OF HIS TRIBE WAS NOT ALL THAT an Apache boy gained when he was admitted to the council. Admission to the council also marked his passing into full manhood. The name given him at birth would be forgotten, and he would win a new one on the warpath. Beyond this, he could now have his own wife and wikiup.

Apaches did not court their wives as white men do. A young warrior could not tell a girl he loved her and wanted her for his wife. He must go to her father and mother and buy her. The price was always in horses. If her people liked him the price was one horse, or maybe two.

The less they liked him, the higher the price they set on their daughter. If they disliked him very much, they set a price which they felt sure he would be unable to pay.

Alope was the prettiest girl in the tribe, and Gokliya felt that, since he would one day be the greatest chief of the Apaches, he should have the prettiest wife. The fact that he owned no horses didn't bother him. Hadn't he already proved himself to be the best of all the Apache boys? Who wouldn't be proud to have him for a son-in-law? As soon as he was admitted to the council he went to see Alope's father and mother.

Old No-po-so and his wife sat at the entrance of their wikiup, watching the newly admitted young warrior strut toward them. Out of sight within, Alope sat beading a soft doeskin moccasin she had made.

Except for the cruelty which already showed in his face, Gokliya was a handsome young warrior. Not tall, he was powerfully built, with broad shoulders, deep chest, narrow hips, and legs that appeared to be sinewed with steel. The fine red blanket that had been his father's hung from one shoulder, his newly won warrior's band was about his head, and every muscle in his body rippled as he came toward the old couple.

At the warrior's council he had not dared do any real fancy bragging, but these old people should know what a fine warrior was offering himself as their son-in-law. With no more than a slight greeting, Gokliya began a flowery, dramatic recital of his great deeds. When his audience seemed unimpressed he let his imagination run wild. Still No-po-so and his wife sat with expressionless faces, their bare feet crossed and their gnarled hands folded in their laps.

Gokliya decided that oratory along would not do, but his imagination was still at work. "I have a very fine horse," he told them, "the swiftest war horse in all the tribe. I will bring it to buy your daughter Alope."

Neither of the old people looked up, but their heads moved slowly from side to side.

"Two horses," Gokliya offered.

The old heads continued to move.

"Three horses! Four!"

Still No-po-so and his wife sat as if half asleep.

Gokliya's anger flared. "I have many horses! Many!" he shouted. "How many horses do you want for your daughter?"

No-po-so glanced at his wife, then leaned slightly forward. Raising all his toes, he held up his fingers behind them. Then he folded his hands again and seemed to be sleeping.

Twenty horses! Any other young warrior would have known he was beaten, but not Gokliya. He had made up his mind that he was going to have Alope for his wife, and neither her people nor anyone else could stop him.

There were plenty of good horses in the horse camps,

and Gokliya had shown how easy it was for him to steal them. But that would be dangerous. Those horses were known, and they belonged to the tribe. If it could be proved that one Apache had stolen from another Apache he could be expelled from the council of warriors. If it could be proved that he had stolen from the tribe he would become an outcast forever.

There was only one thing to do. If No-po-so would not take fewer horses for Alope than he had fingers and toes, then Gokliya must get them as quickly as possible. And there was only one way to get them—steal them from the Mexicans.

The nearest Mexican ranches were more than two hundred miles away. Burning deserts, high mountains and swarms of Mexican cavalry lay between, but these meant nothing to Gokliya. Within half an hour after he left No-po-so's wikiup, he was running steadily and effortlessly southward across the desert.

Gokliya kept running at a steady mile-eating trot until the Big Dipper stood high above the North Star. There was no moon, but he needed none. The long trail before him was as clear in his mind as if he were seeing it in a picture, and he knew exactly where he was going.

This was not the only picture Gokliya could see in his mind. Apaches, particularly the older ones, were great gossips, and No-po-so's wife was one of the greatest. Even now Gokliya imagined her, slipping from wikiup to wikiup, whispering behind her hand and snickering. She and her man had humbled this smart young upstart with the bragging tongue. He, who owned nothing, had come trying to buy Alope. He had strutted and lied and boasted of owning many horses, but No-po-so had fixed him, demanding as many horses as he had fingers and toes.

Anger and injured pride drove Gokliya like a whip. He lengthened his stride and set his jaw. He'd show this gossiping old woman and her insolent husband how much they'd humbled him. Let them gossip and snicker; he'd show them some real humbling! He'd show them and the whole tribe how much their insulting demand meant to the warrior who would one day be their chief.

From earliest childhood, Gokliya's mind had never been idle, his imagination never still. Just as he had planned every detail of attack when scouting an enemy's camp in the hunters' bands, so he had scouted and schemed while with the warriors on his four proving raids.

On their last trip the warriors had tried to raid a big ranch with many fine horses, but had nearly been trapped in an ambush. They had found the horses scattered in herds across a wide valley. At the first sound of alarm Mexican cavalrymen had spurred from canyons to surround the raiders. The Apaches had been lucky to escape with only one warrior killed and one captured.

When the soldiers began shooting, Gokliya dropped flat in his tracks. He lay as if dead while cavalry horses raced almost over him, but his eyes and mind were taking in every detail of the ambush. He realized that the soldiers had been watching for a raid from the north and had been ready for it. But much more important, *all* the soldiers had raced to join the attack, leaving the surrounding canyons unguarded.

As soon as the cavalrymen had raced past him, Gokliya began wriggling for the nearest canyon. When he reached its safety he did not make a run for the meeting place which had been previously arranged, according to Apache custom. There were still many things he wanted to know about that ranch. Slipping like a shadow from boulder to boulder, around deep canyons and over mountain spurs, he circled the whole valley. Before he left he had laid out a plan for a successful raid.

At the south end of the valley there was a deep canyon. Its upper end reached to a pass high on the ridge of the mountains. The canyon walls were tall cliffs, but where the canyon joined the valley it widened, leaving a grassy meadow between the walls. By covering his body with grass, a raider could wriggle across the valley without being seen by the watching soldiers. If he were careful he could move a herd of horses gently into the meadow at the foot of the canyon. The rest would be easy.

If the Apache war whoop were raised at the north end of the valley, the soldiers would all race off to the attack. That would be the moment for the raid. In that high walled canyon the horses could not scatter or turn back. One raider could drive them straight up over the mountain pass and down the other side. The herd could then be circled to the north, and would be far out on the deserts of the Apache homeland before it was ever missed.

Now, as Gokliya ran southward under the stars, every detail of the plan went through his mind again. If he had just one other warrior with him to give the war whoop and draw the cavalrymen away, it would be an easy raid. Alone, he would find it a different matter. He must think of some way to alarm the soldiers and draw them away from the deep canyon. Carefully circling the valley again in his memory, he found the answer.

A little waterfall tumbled down from a high cliff at the north end of the valley. This was just what he needed. After dark he would block the stream at the top of the cliff with a few large rocks. Then he would slip away to gather a herd of horses into the mouth of the big canyon a couple of miles to the south. In a few hours, water backing up behind the rocks would push them over the edge of the cliff, and they would fall with a great clatter. Coming in the night, the noise would stampede any horses nearby. This would be enough to alarm the soldiers and bring them racing to head off a raid.

Gokliya was missing from the tribe for five days. The tongues of the gossips buzzed like a swarm of bees. There was no longer any question about it—No-po-so had shamed this strutting, lying braggart into running away. But he'd be back; there was now no other tribe he could run to. Chief Maco, his grandfather, had died and Hoo had been elected chief in his place. Oh, yes, the big-mouthed one would be back, but he'd have learned his lesson. He'd have to sneak back like a dog with its tail between its legs, and the tribe wouldn't have to listen to his howling after every hunt.

As matters turned out, the gossips were both right and wrong. Gokliya came back, but he didn't come sneaking back. Far from it! He came in a cloud of dust raised by the pounding of two hundred racing hoofs. Mounted on a great war stallion, he drove a whole herd of horses before him, circled them at breakneck speed, and brought them to a stop in front of No-po-so's wikiup.

Within minutes a crowd of astonished onlookers had gathered. The old gossips stood with jaws hanging in dismay. To an Apache a deal was a deal; there was no backing out. Instead of twenty horses, Gokliya had brought fifty! So there was nothing No-po-so could do but let him take Alope.

Old No-po-so had been insulting when he made his demand, but Gokliya was doubly insulting when he paid it. With a show of superb horsemanship he drove his war stallion through the milling horse herd, grasped a beautiful milk-white pony by the mane, and raced with it toward the entrance of the wikiup.

Nearly knocking the bewildered No-po-so and his wife down, Gokliya whirled the horses to a stop at the entrance of the wikiup. This was his moment of triumph and he played it to the limit. Leaping from his horse, he folded his arms across his chest, held his head high, and looked around at the gaping crowd in insolent contempt. Then, without a word, he shouldered past No-po-so, picked up Alope, sat her on the white pony, grasped its mane and dashed away.

This was all the marriage ceremony that was necessary. For four days the couple would be away on a honeymoon. Then they would return. Alope would build a wikiup, and Gokliya would strut before it.

CHAPTER 11

GERONIMO

NO SINGLE APACHE WARRIOR HAD EVER MADE SO successful a raid as Gokliya's, and he expected to become a great hero of his tribe. He might have done so if he had kept his bragging tongue still and had not been so insolent when he returned. But Gokliya had to be the center of attention at any cost. Glory meant more to him than love, honor, food or drink. Since childhood he had taken whatever he wanted by his own skill and daring. When his tribesmen failed to give him the glory he wanted, he tried to take it with his great skill as an actor and orator—strutting, boasting and shouting his own praises.

Failing in this, he determined to become the greatest of

all raid leaders. He would show the whole Apache nation that he should have been chosen instead of Hoo to take his grandfather's place. With his finest oratory he went about trying to raise a large raiding band, but only two young warriors would join him.

Again anger and injured pride whipped Gokliya on. Had he not proved that he could steal horses right out from under the Mexican cavalry's guns? Hadn't he, single-handed, stolen a herd that a whole band of Apache warriors had failed to take? He'd show his sneering tribesmen what a real raider could do.

Still angry, Gokliya led his two followers southward across the deserts. They were afoot, and the pace he set was a killing one. This was to be the quickest and most ruthless raid ever made. He was anxious to get back and strut through the wikiup village with his plunder. This would be no sneaking raid to steal a few horses from a mountain ranch. This would be a raid on a village. He would drive home many pack horses loaded with plunder. He'd be rich, and the envy of every warrior in the tribe.

Even though Gokliya had been unable to convince his tribesmen of his greatness, he was convinced himself. He had nothing but contempt for the Mexicans, and he wasted no time on scouting. Leading his followers boldly into Mexico, he took no care to keep from being seen, passed by unguarded ranches, and hunted for a village with a store and plenty of plunder.

Far to the south he found what he was looking for, but he was just a bit disappointed. True enough, there was a store, and five saddled horses were tied outside, but no man, woman or child was in sight. A raid seemed almost too easy to be exciting. The cowardly Mexicans must have spied him and run to hide in the brush.

Gokliya stopped just long enough to tell his plans hurriedly to his followers. Yelling the Apache war whoop, they would rush the store. He would stand guard while they loaded the plunder on the horses. They need not bother to scatter after the raid, but were to head straight back for their homeland.

Whooping at the top of his lungs, Gokliya led the charge. He had almost reached the store when gunfire blazed from a dozen houses. Ambush! Bullets whizzed past his head and the sound was deafening. Instinct and training alone saved Gokliya. He threw himself flat, rolling and squirming toward a shallow dry ditch. Bullets ripped into the earth around him; flying dirt half blinded him, and sharp stones cut into his skin.

Bleeding but unwounded, Gokliya reached the ditch, rolled in and wriggled like a snake toward the nearest bushes. From their cover he peered back at the village. His two followers lay dead, killed by the first blast of gunfire. Men with guns in their hands were running toward the saddled horses. Others, already mounted, were racing out from behind the houses.

The village lay in a brush-covered, rock-strewn valley. A mile to the east rose the mountains. To the west there were small irrigated fields of grain. Gokliya knew the Mexicans would expect him to run for the mountains, the safest means of escape, so he would go the other way. But first he must hide from the charge that would be upon him within a minute. No nearby bush was big enough to conceal him; he must hide in the open. Well away from any bush, he curled himself into a tight ball—arms, head and legs covered by the curve of his back. His deeply bronzed skin nearly matched the color of the boulders around him, and he kept himself motionless.

The Mexicans knew that Gokliya could not have got far away, and they knew the direction he had taken. Shouting and spurring their horses, they raced toward him, each with his gun cocked and ready. Now was the time for steady nerves. Gokliya did not even let a thought go through his mind. He did not breathe. Every nerve and muscle in him must seem to be as dead as stone.

Fanning out to search behind every bush, the Mexicans bore down upon him. One rider passed so close that his horse's hoof sprayed Gokliya with flying sand. Then they were past, shouting and racing on toward the mountains. Gokliya wasted no time. No horseman would be looking back. Each would be keeping his eyes on the bush ahead. Gokliya ran toward the grain fields, ducking and dodging from bush to bush. Behind him he could hear the excited shouts of the Mexicans. They were nearly to the foothills and knew that he could not have gone that far, that they had missed him somewhere. He could understand no word of their language, but he didn't need to. It was clear that they were spreading out in a wide circle around the village, and would comb every foot of the valley in an attempt to trap him.

Creeping to the nearest irrigation ditch, Gokliya rolled in, wallowed in the soft mud and rubbed it into his hair. When it dried, his body was the exact color of the ground. Listening for the shouts of the Mexicans, he started back toward the safety of the mountains. There was not a minute to waste. The closer the Mexicans tightened their circle, the less chance there would be for him to get through it. Keeping close to the ground, sneaking from bush to bush, wriggling across open spaces, he moved toward the ring of searching horsemen. As he neared it the danger rose. Two or three times a rider passed within less than five yards of him. Each time Gokliya flattened to the ground and lay without thinking or breathing. Then, when he thought the danger was past, a sharp-eyed horseman spied him.

The shot missed. The bullet screeched by Gokliya's ear, but the time for sneaking was past. Horsemen came spurring toward him from both sides and behind. Leaping from side to side so as to make the poorest possible target, Gokliya sprinted for the nearest canyon in the mountains. Behind him galloping hoofs pounded, guns barked, and scores of bullets whistled around him.

Still unwounded, Gokliya reached the mouth of the canyon. It was deep and rough, bush-grown with great spurs of rock jutting from the walls. Gokliya raced for the roughest wall, leaped high into the spurs and found a hiding place among them. While catching his breath he realized that the shouting had stopped. There wasn't even the sound of a horse's hoofs. Had the Mexicans given up? Or were they creeping up on him, covering his hiding place with their guns and waiting for him to make a move?

Cautiously Gokliya shifted his position, keeping his body behind the rock spur, but moving so that he could see up and down the canyon. What he saw was not good from his viewpoint. The Mexicans had left their horses, had again spread out, and were creeping toward him afoot. He was trapped like a rat in a well.

Gokliya flattened himself against the spur and put an arrow to his bowstring. There was only one possible chance of escape. To get a shot at him an enemy would have to climb a jagged rock face. If the enemy could be shot as he reached the top, his body would fall to the bottom of the canyon. All eyes would be drawn toward it, and in that moment a dash for safety could be made.

Minutes dragged slowly by. An eagle circled overhead on soundless wings. The canyon below was as silent. Then

Gokliya's ear caught a faint brushing sound. Bare feet were climbing the jagged rock face, clothing was brushing against the stone. Slowly Gokliya pulled his bowstring—pulled it until the arrowhead rested against the shaft of the bow. And slowly a mat of black hair rose beyond the top of the rock face. Gokliya waited until the head and throat were above the edge. Then his bowstring twanged, the head jerked away into space, and a shot of alarm rang from the canyon floor below. In that moment Gokliya leaped from his hiding place, scaled an almost straight cliff, and bounded over it.

From the canyon came cries of *"Geronimo!" "Geronimo!"* Bullets rang against the cliff around Gokliya, but again he was untouched.

Twice more that day the Mexicans cornered Gokliya. Twice more his bowstring twanged and a Mexicans went down with an arrow in his throat. And twice more Gokliya slipped out of the trap unharmed. Each time the enemy spied him their cry of *"Geronimo!" "Geronimo!"* filled the canyon.

It was their custom to put a Mexican name on any outstanding Indian, and Gokliya had now become important enough to be named.

With the coming of darkness he wriggled through the surrounding ring of Mexicans and cautiously took up the long trail toward his homeland. His great raid had been a terrible failure. All he had to take home was shame—and the name that for forty years would bring terror to the Southwest.

Never again was Gokliya known by any other name than Geronimo. When he returned to his wikiup village he was disliked more than he had been before. The people blamed his headstrong rashness for the loss of his two followers—and some even suspected him of treachery against them. There was nothing for him to brag about, and none would listen to his excuses.

For two months Geronimo brooded and sulked but he did not hang his head in shame. He hunted alone, shared his game with no one, and was haughty and disagreeable to his neighbors. But at the same time he was hunting for any warrior who would go with him on another raid. No warrior of the council would trust him or join him in anything, but at last he found two who had been expelled. They were as anxious as he to redeem themselves.

Again Geronimo led his two followers into Mexico, determined to raid a village and bring home rich plunder.

All the way south Geronimo set too fast a pace. His followers lacked his great endurance, and were exhausted by the time they reached the village he had determined to raid. He planned his attack for dawn, made camp, and went to sleep. Just as he had done before, he held the Mexicans in contempt and did not bother to scout the village or post a lookout.

When dawn came Geronimo found his camp surrounded by Mexicans. He fought like a raging wildcat, broke through the enemy and escaped, but he did not try to save his followers. One was killed. The other escaped, wounded, to find his way back to his homeland alone—and to carry the word of Geronimo's treachery.

CHAPTER 12

CHILDREN OF THE GREAT WHITE FATHER

WHILE GERONIMO WAS MAKING HIS DISASTROUS raids, many great changes were taking place in our country. The Mexican War had been fought and won. Mexico had surrendered California and all the Southwest to the United States.

When General Kearny, guided by Kit Carson, led his army to take command in California, he passed through Apache homeland. Runners brought Chief Mangas Coloradas word of the army's coming and he went to meet it. He was glad to see his old friend Kit Carson again, but was worried by the cannons and the hundred uniformed soldiers. Kit told him there was nothing to fear, that General Kearny was a son of the Great White Father, who lived many days' journey toward the rising sun.

With Kit interpreting, General Kearny and Mangas Coloradas had a long meeting. Mangas sat listening and thinking. General Kearny did all the talking. He said the Great White Father's soldiers were as many as the trees on the mountains, that their big guns spoke with thunder and death. They had whipped the Mexicans, and now the whole Apache homeland belonged to the United States. The General had brought his soldiers to protect the Indians against the enemy, but any Apache who harmed or stole from an American would be killed.

As soon as the meeting was over, General Kearny led his army away toward California, and Mangas Coloradas went to sit in his lonely canyon and think. What was the meaning of all this? Kit Carson had always spoken truth and been a friend of the Apaches. But now he came with talk of a Great White Father and brought a son of that father with great guns and many soldiers.

Who was this Great White Father whose son claimed he had so many soldiers and had whipped the Mexicans? What was this United States to which the Apache homeland was said to belong? Usen had made the homeland for His people before time began, and had given it to them to be theirs forever. The Apaches needed and wanted no protection. Generations ago they themselves had whipped the Mexicans and driven them far to the south.

Why this threat to kill any Apache who harmed or stole from an American? This was insulting. It was big talk for a man to make when he had only a hundred soldiers with him. Five times that number of warriors could be gathered before sunrise. They could easily surround these soldiers and wipe them out. Maybe this was the right time to teach the father of the white men to respect the Apaches and to keep his soldiers and his bragging sons out of the Apache homeland.

Mangas sat thinking for many hours. Maybe he was being too hasty. Kit Carson had always spoken truth. If the father of the white men lived many days' journey toward the rising sun, their homeland must be bigger than the Apaches'. It might be true that their soldiers were as many as the trees on the mountains. Killing Kearny's army might start a long war with an enemy whose strength the Apaches did not know. Maybe this son did not speak for his father. Maybe he was just a big-mouthed talker like Geronimo. At any rate, he had led his soldiers away. It might be best to be patient, to wait for the white men's next move.

Mangas Coloradas did not have to wait long. Soon after the war ended Commissioner Bartlett was sent from Washington to survey the new boundary line between the United States and Mexico. He came into the Apache homeland with quite a party of men, bringing a wagon train, spare horses and mules, and a herd of cattle for food. When Mangas Coloradas heard of his coming he went at once to meet him. Bartlett was a kind and gentle man. Through an interpreter he tried to explain his mission, but Mangas Coloradas found his words more insulting than those of General Kearny.

Yes, Bartlett told him, the Apache homeland now belonged to the United States. He had come to draw a line between it and Mexico. More than this, the Apaches themselves now belonged to the United States. The great father of the white men was now their father, too. He had promised that the Apaches would no longer raid the Mexicans, but would stay on the United States side of the line. And they would give back anything they had already stolen.

Mangas Coloradas shook his head and went away. This was crazy talk. The Apaches belonged only to Usen. He was the Father who had made them and their homeland; they would have no other. What kind of people were these white men who wanted to steal not only the Apache homeland but the people themselves? And what was all this talk about drawing a line? He could see no line! As for the Mexicans . . .

When Mangas Coloradas left Bartlett's camp he was convinced that these white men must be killed if the Apache homeland was to be saved. For two days he rode in silence and in thought. When he reached his stronghold he had changed his mind. A man who dared the spirits to send a blizzard was a fool. The chief who dared an unknown enemy into a war was a bigger fool. These white men must be driven out, but it must be done in a way that would not start a war. These people depended on cattle for food, and on horses for legs. Without them they couldn't live in this country.

Mangas called a few of his trusted warriors and gave them their orders. They were to watch the white men's camp every moment but to make no attack. No white man was to be killed unless he first killed an Apache. No raid was to be made on their stock, but each night four animals were to be separated from their herd and driven far away into the brush.

The warriors did as they were told, and Bartlett went on with his work. Each day he moved his wagons farther along the line he was surveying, and each night his herd dwindled. He did not suspect the Apaches, but thought the stock had wandered away. It didn't matter much; his work was nearly finished.

To Mangas Coloradas it mattered a great deal. When the surveyors were finished and gone, he was sure he had driven them away, and he was very happy. Without doing anything which might have started a war, he had taught white men to stay out of the Apache homeland.

But the lesson had no effect. The boundary was barely

surveyed before American settlers began pouring into this new possession of the United States. These were the pioneers. For three generations they and their forefathers had pushed the American frontier westward—hunting, fighting Indians, and opening new country to civilization. Wherever they could drive their covered wagons they sought out the most fertile valleys and the best hunting grounds in the Apache homeland. If they found Indians in their way they killed them or drove them off.

Mangas Coloradas was worried and deeply troubled. The more he saw of these white men the more he believed they must come from a very strong homeland. His own tribe was now the strongest it had ever been, and his warriors were frantic for revenge, but to start a war with the white men might be disastrous. If they brought great armies of soldiers, the Apaches could be wiped off the earth. It could not be risked. The white men must be driven out, but it must be done just as it had been done with the surveyors. He called a great council of war and told the warriors of his meetings with Kearny and Bartlett. He described how he had driven Bartlett away, and explained his reasons for not wishing to start a war.

Then he laid down his commands: All Mexicans were still the deadly enemies of the Apaches. While the bounties stood, they would raid and kill them as they always had done. All white men would not be raided and killed. Each would be treated as he treated the Apaches. If a white man killed an Apache, an Apache would kill that white man. If he stole deer and elk from the Apaches' hunting grounds, the Apaches would steal cattle and horses from his corrals. There would be no massacres of white people, no killing of women and children—nothing that would give the white men reason to start a war.

Most of the warriors saw the wisdom in their chief's reasoning, just as they had done following the Johnson massacre, but some of the young hotheads were still howling for revenge.

Geronimo sat through the council meeting without a word, and with no expression on his face. Neither he nor his family had been harmed by the frontiersmen, but he believed he could use the white men's ruthlessness to start a rebellion against Mangas Coloradas. If he could stir the warriors into going on the warpath, Mangas would surely be overthrown. Then he, Geronimo, might easily become the new chief of the tribe. As soon as the council ended he went cautiously among the warriors, seeking out the wildest hotheads and whispering to them of a secret meeting.

Word of Geronimo's secret meeting spread, and many more came than even he expected. Now he was getting somewhere! Now he would become the great leader of his people! Leaping onto a high rock at the center of the meeting place, he shouted, "Are we a nation of cowards? Are we a pack of slinking coyotes?"

Spurred on by the yelling of the crowd, Geronimo worked himself into a frenzy, bringing tears to his eyes and the tremble of emotion into his voice. "With the blood of our wives and babies dripping from the white men's knives, our cowardly chief is afraid to fight!" he cried. "He commands us to smile at the white men while they flood our homeland with Apache blood. Will you be ruled by a chief who has long been the friend of white men and the enemy of his own people? Will you obey his commands? Shall we let them steal our homeland? Shall we be their slaves?

"No, my brothers! No!" Geronimo shouted. "A new chief has risen among you—a chief with courage and cunning! Follow him and he will lead you on the glorious warpath. We will kill every white man under the sun and the stars in vengeance for Apache dead. We will all be rich! Rich on the plunder of the white men who would destroy us!

Geronimo paused dramatically. Some of his listeners whooped in wild excitement. Some stood glum, with blank faces. Others shook their heads and scowled. One voice rose above the whooping. "This is treason against our tribe and our chief! Any who join will be expelled from the council! They will be outlaws and outcasts forever!"

Another voice shouted mockingly, "Who is this new chief that would lead us? Is it this great warrior of words? This Geronimo, the great raider who always comes back alone?"

Geronimo was not to be stopped. His voice rose to an angry screech. "Cowards! Women! Go back and hide behind your sniveling chief! Outlaws, are we? Outlaws from slavery! Outcasts? Outcasts from a tribe of cowards!"

On and on went Geronimo's oratory. One by one the warriors slipped away, until only a dozen of the wildest and most bloodthirsty were left. Soon their war whoop was rising around lonely settlers' cabins.

Outcasts from their tribe, Geronimo and his band had little use for plunder, but their thirst for blood and vengeance drove them on like a pack of rabid wolves. Torturing, killing and burning, they raced from cabin to cabin all over the Apache homeland. Their war whoop made the nights hideous—and Geronimo began to gain a little of the fame he had always craved.

CHAPTER 13

COCHISE

EVEN AS MANGAS COLORADAS PLANNED HIS CAMPAIGN against the frontiersmen, another horde of white men was making its way toward the Apache homeland. Gold had been discovered in California. The mountain passes to the north were snow-bound, and the gold-rushers were pushing their wagon trains westward across the deserts. A stage line was established across the southern border of the Apache homeland. Stations were built for feeding and lodging passengers and for keeping relays of fresh horses.

Cochise, the great chief of the southern Apache tribe,

was glad to see the stage lines come. His were the finest warriors among all the Apaches, but they were hunters, not raiders. Their women had few of the pretty things such as Mangas Coloradas' warriors brought home from their raids on the Mexicans. The stage stations needed wood and hay, and the agents paid for it in bright cloth, pots, pans and trinkets. Soon many of the Apache women were busy carrying wood and hay to exchange for the pretty things they wanted. Cochise became a close friend of the agent at the Apache Pass station. He liked and trusted this white man who was honest in his dealings.

With Geronimo's fame spreading, other outlaw Apache bands were formed. Two or three times an outlaw band raided a stagecoach, killed the passengers and stole the horses. Each time, Cochise sent his own warriors to catch the raiders, punish them and bring back the stolen horses.

Not many white settlers had come into Cochise's territory, and those who came had given little trouble. A few of his people had been killed, but his punishment of the killers had been quick and sure. The whites had learned to leave the Indians alone, and the Indians had done the same by them.

To the north an uneven battle was raging. Mangas Coloradas' warriors were carrying out his commands: a white man's life for an Apache life; a white man's horse or cow for an Apache deer or elk. Geronimo and the other outlaws were running wild, raiding, burning and massacring. Unable to tell an outlaw from a good Apache, the frontiersmen were shooting at every Indians they saw, but they were almost helpless. If they hunted game to feed their families their horses and cattle were stolen. If they fought to defend their stock they were cut down by arrows from ambush. In terror they demanded that the United States government send cavalry to protect them.

Forts were built and large companies of cavalry were sent into the Apache homeland, but the soldiers were nearly as helpless as the settlers. Few of the officers had experience in Indian warfare; none knew the Apache system of ambush, lightning attack and fadeaway escape. There were some excellent officers, but others believed that the only good Indians were dead ones. Little effort was made to find the guilty; the first Apache they came upon was punished or killed.

Mangas Coloradas set his jaw and kept his command in force. For every Apache killed by a soldier, an arrow from ambush picked a cavalryman out of his saddle.

In February 1861, a young lieutenant named Bascom, recently graduated from military school, was given his first command against the Apaches. He was sent out to find and punish a band of raiders who had stolen a Mexican boy and a few cattle from a ranch near the stage line. Here was his chance to make himself a reputation in a hurry. He'd heard that Chief Somebody-or-other often came to the nearby stage station. He'd give this cowardly, thieving chief a lesson he wouldn't soon forget. Taking a small detachment of cavalrymen, he rode boldly to Apache Pass.

By chance, Cochise, his brother and two nephews were nearby when the lieutenant and his force arrived. Cochise had never seen uniformed soldiers and decided to go and make friends with them. The lieutenant had other ideas. He at once demanded that Cochise return the boy and cattle he had stolen. When the Chief said he knew nothing of the theft, Lieutenant Bascom accused him of lying. Then, over the protests of the agent, he ordered Cochise and his relatives seized and thrown into a strongly guarded tent.

This was the greatest insult that could have befallen an Apache chief, but Cochise didn't lose his temper. This was a boy soldier, and boys were apt to be impulsive. It would be best to handle this in a way that would avoid trouble between the soldiers and the Apaches. Waiting for dark, Cochise slit the tent and raced for the nearest canyon. The soldiers shot wildly, and Cochise escaped with only a slight wound. Within an hour he could have gathered enough warriors to wipe out the lieutenant's force, but he had other plans. Even a boy soldier would understand an exchange of prisoners.

Next morning, Cochise came to within shouting distance of the station. A few of his warriors were holding two Americans, and Cochise shouted that he was ready to exchange prisoners.

The lieutenant became furious. Though he had seized his prisoners without cause and through treachery, he refused to make the exchange, demanding instead that the Americans be released immediately. Cochise demanded that his relatives be released first, since they had been taken first. The agent, the captured Americans, and his own sergeant pleaded with Bascom to let his prisoners go, but he was adamant. Threats were shouted back and forth between the Chief and the headstrong young lieutenant. Tempers flared to white heat. Before they cooled, the Apaches had killed their prisoners and Bascom had hanged Cochise's relatives—starting the greatest Indian war in history.

Within an hour runners were on the trails to every corner of Apacheland. The chiefs of all nine Apache tribes, together with their finest warriors, were to gather at Cochise's stronghold on the rising of the fifth sun.

The fifth sunrise found Cochise's stronghold thronged. Guns rested across a thousand arms; bows and spears bristled above two thousand shoulders. Nine chiefs sat alone, with their heads together. Their decision might spell life or death for the whole Apache nation. There must be no snap judgment. They must not allow anger to lead them onto a warpath that could bring only death and destruction to their people. On the other hand, they must not allow fear or caution to keep them from the warpath if it were necessary to save their people from slavery.

The sun was near its setting when the chiefs rose and Cochise mounted the great rock at the center of his stronghold. He had been chosen war chief of the whole nation; he would speak for all the chiefs. The warriors crowding around him covered the mountaintop. Cochise stood with his head bowed, his arms folded across his chest. His deeply bronzed body seemed to be a statue from which dignity, strength and calm flowed over his troubled people. They waited in awed silence for his words. In the stillness, the song of a thrush rose clear and sweet on the evening air.

Slowly Cochise raised his head and spread his arms. His deep voice rolled out to the farthest edges of the crowd. "My brothers, we have come to the place where our path branches like the horns of the young deer. To the right is the path of peace and slavery. To the left is the path of war and blood. No man setting his feet on the warpath can see its ending. It may lead a whole people into the land of the spirits—the land of the dead and forgotten. Or it may lead to the freedom our fathers knew. We must choose which path our feet will follow.

"Many summers and winters we have followed the single path. We have tried to walk as brothers with the white men. Many of them have walked behind us on the narrow path and have thrust a knife between our ribs. The path is lined with the bodies of Apache dead. A few white men have walked in peace and honesty; they have been friends to the Apaches.

"The bee is the friend of the Apache. Its honey is sweet to his taste. The hornet is the Apache's enemy. It makes no honey but stings his children and drives them from the wikiup. Will a man let a swarm of hornets nest in his wikiup because there are a few bees among them?

"The white men talk of their great father who lives beyond the rising sun. They tell us he is the friend of the Apaches. But he sends his favorite sons to insult us and try to frighten us. They brag of his soldiers who are as many as the trees on the mountains and of his big guns that speak with a thousand deaths. One tells us our homeland belongs to his father. Another, that we ourselves belong to him. He sends a boy soldier to capture our chiefs by treachery and to throw them like slaves into a prison. He sends his hunters to kill the deer and elk that Usen has given us to feed our children. He sends his soldiers to kill our peaceful hunters on the trail.

"Are these the acts of a friend who loves us, or of an enemy who would destroy us? Shall we walk the path of peace and slavery, or shall we put our feet upon the warpath?"

Cochise paused while the cry for war swelled to a thundering roar. Turning slowly, with arms spread wide and palms lifted, he stilled his warriors. "The great bull elk of the mountains is a mighty warrior. At his bellow the panther and the bear slink from his path. Yet, my brothers, he runs in terror from the stinging wasp. His bellow does not frighten it away. His ripping hoofs and antlers are as blades of grass against its darting strikes.

"The white man is a mighty warrior. In battle his strength is as the raging fire that kills the forests. The bellow of his big gun roars like a thousand bulls. His gun shoots far and straight. Yet, my brothers, he will run from the sting of the wasp. What he cannot see he cannot harm.

"The brave bear that faces the bull elk in battle feeds many coyotes. The wasp that stings and darts away lives to sting many times again. You are brave, my warriors, but the brave in battle sleep long in a hero's grave.

"Many summers ago Mangas Coloradas' people gathered to feast with the white man. A great gun blasted them as fire blasts the trees of the forest. We cannot see beyond the rising sun. We cannot see into the homeland of the white man. We cannot see how many big guns are in his wikiup. We cannot see if his soldiers are as many as the trees on all the mountains. The Apache warriors are only as many as the trees on one mountain.

"If there are ten mountains in a homeland and fire kills the trees on one, the loss is as nothing. If the trees on our one mountain are killed the Apaches will be no more. They will sleep in the grave of a forgotten people. We will not fight the white man in battle, where the fire of his great guns can burn us down. In little bands we will sting and drive him as the wasp drives the bull elk. For every tree that falls on the mountain of the Apaches, ten must fall on the mountains of the white men. For every Apache killed in the fire of war ten whites must die.

"We have no guns that speak with a thousand deaths. We can make no guns that speak with a single death. The arrows of the Apaches do not speak. Their whisper is lost in the singing of the wind. They make no smoke to tell from which bush they flew. But their sting is as deadly as the bullet.

"Go, my brothers! Drive the white men from among us, that our children may walk in freedom through the homeland Usen has made for them."

CHAPTER 14

GERONIMO AND THE COCHISE WAR

LONG BEFORE THE WHITE MEN CAME, THE APACHES had a signal system by which they could send messages. During the Cochise War it was developed to so fine an art that it was almost equal to our telegraph. On every high mountain in Apachcland lookouts and signalmen were kept posted. Each puff of smoke by day or flicker of firelight by night carried a message. Within a few hours it could be relayed as much as five hundred miles.

Though the Apaches had no written language, they had post offices. Each stick poked into a pile of stones beside a trail had its meaning, and every Apache warrior could read it.

At his stronghold, Cochise held the reins of war tightly in his hands. Stealthy as foxes, his scouts slipped from cover to cover throughout the homeland, watching every company of soldiers, wagon train, stagecoach, traveler and settler. The white men's actions were reported by sticks poked into the stones of a post office. Soon the message would be read by a passing runner and carried to the nearest signal station. In puffs of smoke or flickers of light, it was sent from mountaintop to mountaintop until it reached the stronghold.

There Cochise planned his campaign and sent out his commands. There was to be no general massacre of the whites, but a steady harassment that would drive them out of the Apache homeland. Bands of ten to fifteen warriors were scattered all over the homeland. At a signal from high on a mountaintop a band would strike a certain wagon train or settler's ranch. Horses and cattle were killed; wagons, buildings and haystacks burned, and growing crops destroyed. Most of the attacks were made at the crack of dawn. They were lightning-fast and seldom lasted more than a few minutes. Then the warriors scattered into the dimness. But Cochise's first policy was always carried out, for every Apache who lost his life ten white men were killed.

With the beginning of the Cochise War, the United States government rushed more troops into the Apache homeland. At each report of an attack, commanders sent a force of cavalry racing to punish the attackers. This was exactly what Cochise wanted. He would keep the soldiers so busy they would have no time for attacking the wikiup villages.

At dawn a plume of smoke would rise from a burning ranch, stagecoach or wagon train, and soldiers would be sent racing to the scene. Before they reached it, another plume would rise fifty miles away. Again the soldiers would dash off madly to catch and punish the attackers. But more often than not, it was the white men who were punished. If an Apache warrior was killed in an attack and there were not enough white men there to keep the score even at ten to one, the soldiers were ambushed.

The only road through the Apache homeland was the stage road. Elsewhere the trails were narrow and cavalry had to ride single file across brush-covered deserts, through deep canyons, and over forested mountain passes. Every bush, tree and boulder was a perfect hiding place for an Apache warrior. With their bronze-colored bodies motionless against the red-brown of the desert, a band of warriors could lie within ten feet of a trail and be invisible to the soldiers. Then, as the file of cavalry passed, arrows would whisper from tight-drawn bowstrings.

Trying to fight an enemy they could not see was maddening to the soldiers. In frustration, some of the more hot-headed young officers took out their spite on any Apache they found—old men, women, or even children.

This Cochise had expected, and he had an answer ready for it. Apache outcasts were never allowed to go on the warpath with the warriors, but now the time had come when the outlaw bands must be used. If the white men was going to use terror, treachery and massacre, the Apaches would do the same. Smoke signals rose from every mountaintop; Geronimo and all the other outcast leaders were asked to join the war against the white enemy.

This was the day Geronimo had waited for. Now he would prove that he was the greatest war chief among the Apaches! Now he could commit any atrocity against the hated whites without fear of punishment from his own people. Now he would become the most famous Indian in the world!

There was no limit to Geronimo's drive and cruelty. With less than forty followers he devastated south-central Arizona. Racing from ranch to ranch, from frontier cabin to cabin, he tortured, murdered and burned. No white person—man, woman or child—was spared.

Soon the cry of *"Geronimo!" "Geronimo!"* was the most terrifying sound in the Southwest. Frantic messages were sent from Washington. Geronimo must be captured or killed at any cost. If necessary, the entire cavalry force must be withdrawn from the Cochise War and put on his trail.

Nothing could have pleased Geronimo more. Now he had become important! Now he was gaining the fame he had always craved! The torturing and killing of helpless settlers was no longer enough to feed his ego. Now he would prove that he was not only the smartest Apache but also smarter than any white man. He took great care to commit his worst atrocities when a large force of cavalry was hot on his trail.

The International Boundary was an imaginary line drawn between the United States and Mexico. Under the law, the soldiers of one country could not cross the line into the territory of the other. Geronimo was the first Apache to discover this, and the first to learn where the line ran. He made full use of his knowledge, and the daring of his raids became unbelievable.

Almost within sight of a strongly garrisoned United States cavalry post, he would commit one of his most horrible crimes. Making no attempt to escape, he would let his little band be completely surrounded by several hundred cavalrymen. Then, waiting until they believed they at last had him cornered, he would suddenly escape.

Sometimes it was in a bold, driving charge through the weakest part of the line. Sometimes he would abandon his horses, scatter his followers, and sneak them out almost under the hoofs of the cavalry mounts. With the soldiers still beating the bushes and hunting him inside their trap, he would gather his warriors, steal fresh horses, and race across the line. From the Mexican side he would insult the soldiers with shouts and signals, daring them to come over and get him.

Geronimo was not only the first Apache to make use of the boundary line but probably the first to discover the usefulness of field glasses. This was hard on the cavalry officers, whose field glasses made them a prime target for Geronimo's ambushes. Goading a small force of cavalry into a chase, he would lead it into a well-prepared ambush. An officer carrying field glasses was indeed fortunate to come out of the ambush alive.

All the guns which the Apaches had taken in their raids on Mexico were powder-and-ball muskets, but some United States cavalry units were armed with rifles and cartridges. It did not take Geronimo long to discover that these were far more accurate, deadlier and quicker to reload than muskets. From that time on his ambushes were laid for cavalry units that carried rifles.

Armed with his wonderful memory for terrain, his skill at setting and escaping ambushes, the Apache signal system, high-powered field glasses, rifles and plenty of ammunition, Geronimo had absolute contempt for American soldiers. From mountaintops his lookouts watched the cavalry with glasses; from hiding places within fifty yards, his scouts watched every army post. Each move the soldiers made was told in puffs of smoke that rose against the sky. Each ambush the Americans set was turned into an ambush on themselves.

Geronimo was in his glory. More than two thousand United States soldiers were wearing their mounts to skin and bones chasing after him. Meanwhile, he laughed in their faces, killed them off like flies, and goaded them on by committing crimes under their very noses. His fame was spreading; his name was becoming known all over the West.

In the meantime, Cochise and his warriors were carrying on a relentless war against the settlers. The Chief had kept his score at ten to one, and the white men were unable to withstand the pressure. One after another, covered wagons made their way north and east, out of the Apache homeland. The stage line no longer ran. Ranches, mines and settlements were abandoned. Then the soldiers began to leave. Cochise, Mangas Coloradas and the other chiefs believed they had whipped the Americans and forced them to withdraw their soldiers.

But unknown to the Apaches, the Civil War had broken out. Both officers and enlisted men were quitting their posts and going to join the armies of the Union or the Confederacy. Pressed for cavalry, the War Department in Washington recalled units from Indian service for engagement in the war.

Now was the time, the Apache chiefs decided, to make a clean sweep of every remaining white man in the Apache homeland. They redoubled their efforts.

CHAPTER 15

THE BATTLE OF
APACHE PASS

WITH ALMOST EVERY AMERICAN DRIVEN FROM Apacheland, the chiefs called their warriors home from the warpath. Each day it was becoming harder to find a living for the women and children. The settlers had nearly stripped the homeland of deer and elk. Those that had not been killed had been frightened far back into the high mountains, and the warriors were needed for hunting.

Hoo, chief of the tribe that had been Maco's, was a cruel and treacherous drunkard. Under his leadership the whole tribe had turned into a great gang of bandits. He had joined the Cochise War to raid and plunder the Americans.

As the settlers left Apacheland the raiding became poor, so Hoo moved his tribe into Mexico. There they raided far to the south, killing to satisfy their lust for blood, torturing, plundering, burning and getting drunk on stolen wine. It was not long before Geronimo and his band of outlaws joined Hoo's tribe. Soon they too had become a band of drunkards.

In the early summer of 1862, a regiment of California Volunteers was equipped with the latest models of breechloading rifles and shellfiring howitzers, then ordered to join the Union forces in Texas. General J. H. Carlton, its commander, planned to march eastward by the shortest route—across Southern Arizona and through Apache Pass.

The California regiment had no sooner entered Arizona than Apache scouts flashed news of its coming to Cochise. He was deeply worried. Here was an army that outnumbered his own warriors many times over, and it was marching fearlessly into the Apache homeland. He could only believe that it had been sent to take the homeland away from the Apaches. The army must be stopped, but he could not cope with it alone. So, while his scouts kept constant watch of the approaching army, he sent a swift runner to bring his friend Mangas Coloradas, the greatest strategist among all American Indians.

Together the two great chiefs sat pondering and listening to the reports that scouts brought in each hour. The soldiers were marching straight toward Cochise's stronghold, high in the mountains above Apache Pass. There could be no question about it; the Americans had sent this army to rob the Apaches of their homeland. It must be defeated, but how? There were not enough warriors in all the Apache tribes to defeat it in open battle, and few of those with guns had ammunition for them. Some other plan must be found.

While Cochise sent runners far and wide to gather the finest warriors, Mangas Coloradas began forming his plans. Hour after hour he sat alone at the summit of Apache Pass, thinking and gazing off across the dry alkali desert that stretched for forty miles to the westward. Beyond the desert were the sulphur springs, and two days' march beyond the springs was the advancing army. He must think how the white chief leading that army would reason, and how his soldiers could be defeated with the very least loss of Apache lives. There was no possibility of defeating them with bullets; they must be defeated with thirst—thirst and surprise.

The Cochise stronghold could be reached from the west only by way of Apache Pass which rose, funnel-shaped, from the desert. The pass was rough and boulder-strewn. Near its summit, high cliffs crowded in to form a narrow canyon. At their base a spring of clear, cool water bubbled, but there was not another drop to be found between there and Sulphur Springs, forty miles westward across a blistering desert. The chief of the soldiers would have to water his men and horses at the sulphur springs, then push on rapidly to water again at the head of Apache Pass. If he could be held away from the water in the pass for one extra day, his men and horses would die of thirst in the desert. In that heat they would never live to get back to Sulphur Springs. Every hour they could be delayed would weaken their ability to fight.

By the time the warriors were gathered the California regiment had reached Sulphur Springs, and Mangas Coloradas had his strategy well planned. Where Apache Pass narrowed into a canyon, great boulders were rolled to the edges of the cliffs, ready to be toppled off onto the heads of any soldiers who might get that far. The best riflemen among the warriors were hidden in crevices high in the rock walls. There they would be safe from enemy rifle fire and able to rain bullets down on the soldiers in the pass.

Farther down, bowmen were concealed behind boulders close to the trail, where their whistling arrows could pick cavalrymen out of their saddles. Behind a spur of the mountain, out of sight of the trail, a hundred warriors were stationed on their swiftest ponies, ready to strike and dash away before their fire could be returned.

Mangas had spent many hours in watching American soldiers from hiding. No one knew their fighting ability better than he, but he had noticed that they were careless when no fight was expected. They did not keep their ranks well formed, were not always alert, and could not read the mountain and desert signs of danger as Apaches could. If their officers' suspicions were not aroused the soldiers might stumble into the trap in small companies. This would make the task of ambushing them safer and easier.

Mangas called his warriors together and gave them their orders: No Apache must let himself be seen, or make a sound that could be heard by the soldiers. No shot was to be fired until the soldiers were well advanced into the pass and until he himself raised the Apache war whoop. Then every bullet and every arrow must be made to count. If the soldiers retreated they were not to be followed. Every warrior was to stay in his hiding place to meet the next advance. They did not need to kill all the soldiers—thirst in the desert would do that—but they must not allow them to reach the spring at the summit of the pass. The soldiers had big guns that would speak with the voice of thunder, but the Apaches were not to be afraid of them. Big guns could not kill warriors who could not be seen.

Since sunrise the California regiment has marched nearly forty waterless miles under a blistering July sun. Cavalry horses shuffled through the alkali dust with their heads hung low. Soldiers, with their canteens empty and their mouths as dry as the dust under their burning feet, shuffled along behind. The nearly exhausted regiment was strung out for miles along the deserted Butterfield stage road when Captain Roberts' advance guard reached the foot of Apache Pass.

It was a straggling advance guard, made up of 300 infantrymen, a troop of cavalry and two howitzers. No Indians had been seen since the column entered Arizona, and Captain Roberts had grown careless. He had neglected to put out either flankers or scouts. An Apache would have known by the stillness of the birds that an enemy was in hiding close by. But Captain Roberts was not interested in bird songs; he was interested only in reaching water at the summit of Apache Pass. Looking neither to right nor left, he led his straggling troops up the steep, boulder-lined roadway that wound toward the narrow canyon at the head of the pass.

The soldiers were two-thirds of the way up to the spring when Mangas Coloradas raised the wild Apache war whoop. Seven hundred warriors joined in the blood-chilling yell. The echoing canyon walls threw it back in an ear-shattering screech. Rifles barked and chattered from the cliffs on both sides of the gorge. Bullets and arrows raked through human and animal flesh. Men and horses shrieked in pain and panic.

Just in time to avert a complete massacre, Captain Roberts shouted the order to retreat. Mangas and his mounted warriors raced in to take their toll as the bewildered soldiers ran, stumbling and tumbling, down to the desert.

Captain Roberts had been careless and had failed to use his head, but for all that he was a brave and brilliant soldier. He knew that water must be obtained soon or the regiment would be lost. With his advance guard, he would have to fight a way through to the spring. Quickly re-forming his command, he placed the two howitzers at the head of the column and again marched into the pass.

The second Apache attack was even fiercer than the first, but this time Captain Roberts held his troops in formation, returning fire at every puff of gun smoke from the canyon walls. With the two howitzers at the front, he pushed his ranks forward toward the summit of the pass—and water.

The only Indians to be seen were a few on top of the cliffs, out of rifle range but poised and ready to roll boulders down on the heads of the advancing troops. The narrow neck of the canyon could not be forced until these Indians were cleared from the cliff tops. Captain Roberts withdrew to a point where he could bring his howitzers into bearing, then lobbed explosive shells up onto the cliffs.

From below he could not see the slaughter that these bursting shells were causing on the cliff tops. But he could not help seeing the slaughter that Apache bullets and arrows were causing around him. Night was coming on and he doubted his ability to win through to the spring without reinforcements. Calling to a few cavalrymen, he sent them racing back to warn the rest of the regiment and hurry it along.

Mangas Coloradas knew what the cavalrymen's mission must be as soon as he saw them race down through the canyon. They must be headed off or killed before their message was delivered. Shouting to his best mounted warriors to follow, he whipped away in pursuit of the messengers.

The swift Indian ponies gained rapidly on the tired cavalry mounts. Trooper John Teal's horse stumbled and nearly fell from exhaustion. Teal pulled it off the trail, hoping the Indians would pass him by. But Mangas Coloradas would not chance letting a single messenger escape. He and his warriors could stop to kill this soldier and still have plenty of time to overtake the others.

Teal's mount was killed by the first Apache shot. The young trooper sprawled headlong, but held onto his rifle and crawled back behind his fallen horse.

Mangas knew nothing of the new breechloading rifles. He shouted to his warriors to draw the trooper's shot, then rush him when his gun was empty. But Teal was never caught with an empty rifle. Firing as fast as he could flip the breech, he sent a stream of bullets at the circling Indians. One particularly big Indian caught his eye. He jerked his rifle sights toward the giant Indian and pulled the trigger.

Mangas Coloradas pitched from his saddle and lay

motionless on the ground, a great gaping hole ripped through his chest.

Teal was forgotten by the warriors, who leaped from their ponies and crowded around their fallen chief. Mangas Coloradas, though well past seventy years of age and desperately wounded, was still alive. But the Apache warriors had no will to fight without him to lead them. They lifted him gently, laid him on a stretcher of mesquite bows and, running with their burden all night, took the chief to the nearest doctor, in Janos, Mexico.

When the news was carried back to the warriors in Apache Pass, the firing stopped and the Apaches slipped away through the darkness. The Battle of Apache Pass was over—won by John Teal, a boy trooper still in his teens.

CHAPTER 16

THE PEACE TREATY

WHEN WORD REACHED THE EAST THAT THE APACHES had attacked a whole regiment of United States soldiers, the people were appalled. They demanded that the government bring these bloodthirsty savages under control, and the California Volunteers were given the task. Their commanding general believed there was one way of controlling the Apaches. His orders were: "The men are to be slain whenever and wherever found; women and children may be taken prisoners."

The soldiers followed their general's order about slaying Apache men, but they paid no attention to the part about taking prisoners. In small companies they scoured the mountains and deserts like hunters of dangerous wild beasts and killed any Apache found. Not a single prisoner was taken in eight years.

Following the disastrous Battle of Apache Pass, Cochise continued his war against the white men, but the other chiefs did not join him. They hid their people deep in the mountains trying to protect them from the soldiers. Without their help Cochise could no longer carry on his war in every part of the Apache homeland. He drew back into the territory which had been his before the coming of the white men, and the soldiers left it strictly alone.

But if Cochise and his warriors were too dangerous to be attacked, there was no letup on the less war-like tribes. As a result, the chiefs hid their people away deeper and deeper in the mountains. The fertile valleys of Apacheland again became safe for white men, and American settlers began returning to them. Many were settlers who had been driven out at the beginning of the Cochise War. As they returned they joined the soldiers in hunting down and killing the hated Apaches.

Mangas Coloradas, at last recovered from his wound, was deeply worried. He realized that the Apaches could never withstand the power of the white men and their modern weapons. If war continued between them, the Apaches would soon be a forgotten people. He must convince the tribes of this. So, although in frequent pain from his wound, he hunted out and talked to every Apache chief except Hoo. Cochise would not give up, but all the others were willing to accept the white men in their homeland if their people were allowed to live in peace.

Mangas Coloradas knew the risk he was taking, but his life was nearly spent, and the good he might be able to do was well worth the risk. Under what he believed to be an invitation from the commander at Fort McLean, he went there for a peace talk. Unfortunately, the invitation was a trap, and the commander was one who believed that the only good Indians were dead ones. He had Mangas seized and thrown into a guarded tent. As he walked way, he turned back to the guards and said, "I want him dead or alive tomorrow morning; do you understand? *I want him dead!*"

The commander got what he wanted—and for several years the Cochise War flamed anew. Cochise struck hard and swiftly, attacking army posts and cutting a bloody swath through the white settlers of central Arizona. Hoo brought his raiders north from Mexico to murder, burn and pillage. Geronimo ran wild. No atrocity was too horrible for him to commit against the whites. In lightning dashes across the Mexican border, he terrorized the whole of southern Arizona.

The soldiers and settlers were unable to cope with the fierceness of Cochise's warriors or the wanton raids of Geronimo and Hoo. In rage and frustration some of the settlers turned to treachery. Messages were sent to two of the most peace-loving chiefs, inviting them to bring their people in from the mountains and smoke the pipe of peace. The chiefs brought them in, and the white men made them peaceful Indians—by killing them.

President Grant was deeply shocked when word reached him that peaceful Apaches were being massacred by the settlers. He demanded that the leaders of the massacre mobs be tried for murder, and threatened to put Arizona Territory under martial law. Then he sent an agent to investigate the whole Apache problem.

On his return the agent reported that the Apaches must have reservations where they would be fed and protected by the government. The white settlers had taken all the best land and killed most of the deer and elk. The Indians were forced either to starve or to raid the white settlers for enough food to keep themselves alive.

However, the Arizona settlers were still being terrorized by Geronimo, and they demanded that the government send enough soldiers to kill all the Apaches. President Grant selected General Howard and sent him to Arizona with full authority to act for the United States government. His mission was to find Cochise and make a treaty of peace with him. Then he was to stop Geronimo's raiding and set up reservations where the Apaches could be fed and protected.

At the same time the President transferred General

Crook to Arizona. General Crook was famous for his firmness in handling Indians, as well as for his understanding of them. He was also noted for his courage, honesty and fairness. The General was instructed to gather the Apaches onto reservations and to see that they were protected from white treachery. Agents would then be sent from the Bureau of Indian Affairs to take care of feeding and clothing the reservation Apaches.

In spite of Cochise's distrust of the white men, his closest friend was a Yankee frontiersman named Tom Jeffords. For many years Cochise had admired and trusted him. He was the only white man who knew where the chief's stronghold was or who had ever been in it.

When General Howard arrived in Arizona he went straight to Tom Jeffords. With Jeffords' help he was able to meet Cochise. At the time of the meeting Cochise was in his middle seventies, and his only remaining sons were in their early teens. Cochise knew there was no warrior in the tribe who was wise and powerful enough to lead his people in war after his death. Peace must be made with the white men, but he was determined that his own tribe should not be harmed by the treaty terms.

Cochise sat long in stony silence, studying this white man. He was trying to discovery if the General spoke with a double tongue, if he actually had authority to make promises which the United States government would keep. At last he was convinced of General Howard's sincerity and honesty. Within a few days he laid down the only treaty terms he would agree to, and General Howard accepted them for the United States government.

Under the terms of the treaty, Cochise would leave the warpath and, if necessary, would use his own warriors to stop Hoo's and Geronimo's raids upon the Americans. In exchange, his tribe was to be given all of its homeland as a reservation, forever. Tom Jeffords was to be appointed agent. He would be supplied with whatever food and clothing were needed and would be responsible to no one except the chief of the Indian Bureau. No other white man, either soldier or settler, was to be allowed on the reservation. It would be the United States Army's responsibility to keep them off.

Neither Geronimo nor Hoo wanted peace, and they were furious at the terms to which Cochise had agreed. Hoo was all for defying the old chief and continuing raids on the Americans, but Geronimo knew this would be too dangerous. Cochise had given his word; he would not go back on it. And his punishments were quick and severe. Besides, Geronimo had a better plan.

The treaty had barely been made when Geronimo presented himself to General Howard as the chief of Hoo's tribe. He said his people had become a part of Cochise's tribe at the beginning of the long war. They had always been friends of the white men, and were glad that peace had finally been made. All they wanted was to come and live on the new reservation, and to be protected, fed and clothed by their Great White Father. The General was much pleased, and told Geronimo that he and his people would be welcome.

The southern boundary of the new reservation was the line between the United States and Mexico. Next morning Hoo's tribe began building a dozen or so wikiup villages, all of them just within the United States side of the boundary. Here lived the old people, women and children of the tribe. But the warriors had their camp hidden away deep in the roughest and wildest mountains of Mexico. With their dependents now clothed and fed by the United States government, the warriors had all their time free for the warpath. More than this, they had a stronghold which the Mexican cavalry could not break through—the International Boundary.

From this time on Geronimo was definitely the brains and spokesman for the tribe of which his grandfather had been chief. For two years he and Hoo and their bandits devastated northern Mexico, even going as far south and west as the Gulf of California. The Mexican government increased its cavalry tenfold, but the soldiers were helpless. If they picked up the outlaw's trial and pressed it hard, Geronimo made a dash over the border to safety inside the reservation. There, posing as peaceful Indians, the outlaws drew rations, clothing and new blankets from the United States government. Jeffords, with nearly two thousand Indians to take care of, could not keep track of or control them.

In the meantime, General Crook was making good progress in bringing Apaches onto other reservations. But he was unable to get them clothed and fed when he brought them in. A gang of dishonest settlers, traders and politicians had set up a scheme for cheating the government and the Apaches. The swindlers were known as the Tucson Ring. They had strong political power and demanded that they have the choosing of the Indian agent in Arizona.

It was the Indian agent who placed orders for the food, blankets and clothing needed on the reservations. When the goods were delivered, it was the agents' duty to inspect them, approve the bills and send them to Washington for payment. The Tucson Ring would appoint only agents who would order goods from members of the ring and who would approve and send bills for payment even when no delivery had been made. This, of course, left the Apaches on the reservation to freeze and starve.

When General Crook fought against this dishonesty, the Tucson Ring succeeded in having him transferred out of Arizona.

CHAPTER 17

THE APACHE POLICE

EXCEPT FOR THOSE ON THE COCHISE RESERVATION, the Apaches in Arizona were soon as badly off as when President Grant first heard of their plight. If they came in to the reservations they were robbed and starved by the Tucson Ring. If they raided and stole from the whites to keep their families alive, they were trailed down and killed by the soldiers. There was only one answer to the problem: an agent must be sent to Arizona whom the Tucson Ring could neither control nor corrupt. The Dutch Reformed Church was asked to suggest a man, and chose John P. Clum.

John Clum was twenty-two years old when, in 1874, he was sent to Arizona as agent at the San Carlos Reservation. Before accepting the appointment he demanded, and was promised, full control of the reservation. He had no experience with Indians, but was absolutely fearless, honest, farsighted, and had a keen understanding of human nature. He did not look down on the Apaches, but considered them his equals in every way.

It took John Clum a very short time to win the confidence of the Apaches near San Carlos and to learn their language. It took him an even shorter time to earn the hatred of the Tucson Ring. He would approve no bill until the full measure of goods had been delivered, and he insisted that the quality be equal to the price.

The army commandant who had been appointed to take General Crook's place felt that it was his duty to control all the Apaches in Arizona. John Clum disagreed. He insisted that he had been given full control of the reservation and would stand for no interference by the soldiers. It was only natural that this brought him the ill will of the Army. The General withdrew his troops far from San Carlos. He'd teach this young upstart a lesson! The last agent had been mauled and driven away by the Indians. A taste of the same medicine would be good for this big-headed boy.

But John Clum believed the Apaches were capable of self-government, and set about to prove it. Calling the people together, he told them that if they could make good laws, enforce them, punish wrongdoers and keep peace on the reservation, he would never let the soldiers interfere. Then he organized an all-Apache court and police force.

The reservation Apaches were eager to prove that they could govern themselves and took great pride in their court and police force. With Clum as judge and twelve of the wisest leaders as jury, they passed laws very much like ours, tried wrongdoers and set punishments. The police force kept watch over the whole reservation, arrested those who broke the laws, and carried out the punishments set by the court.

There had never been more than seven hundred Apaches on the San Carlos Reservation before John Clum came there. But word of his honesty and fair dealing spread quickly. Within a few months the number of Indians there was above a thousand; within a year it was above four thousand. Now the number was too great to be handled by an untrained police force. Clum began hunting for the right white man to lead and train the Apache police. He was fortunate in finding Clay Beauford, a former cavalryman who spoke the Apache language, inspired Indians and was a natural leader.

Choosing the best twenty-five men of the Apache police, Beauford decked them out in whatever scraps of uniform could be found, armed them with good rifles, taught them drill formations and paid them a few dollars a month. The Apache police quickly became an excellent drill team, and every young warrior on the reservation longed for a place on the force. Within a few months the number of Apache police was increased to a hundred, and they became the finest law-enforcement body in the Southwest.

While conditions improved in San Carlos, they went from bad to worse on the Cochise reservation. Cochise was dying. Tom Jeffords had lost interest, and trouble was afoot. Many of Cochise's young warriors, tired of idleness on the reservation, had joined the outlaws. Geronimo was stirring up trouble wherever he could, plotting against the sons of the old chief, and trying to start an uprising against the whites.

At Cochise's death the smoldering fire burst into flame. In April 1876, there was an outbreak. An overland stage was attacked, white men were killed, houses burned and livestock stolen. Again southern Arizona was in terror. The cavalry was sent to capture and punish the raiders, but was unable to catch them.

Early in May the Commissioner of Indian Affairs telegraphed Clum from Washington. He was to take over the Cochise reservation and remove the Apaches from there to San Carlos if it seemed best.

Clum knew he could not do this without the support of his Apache court and police force. He called the leaders together and explained the matter to them. For a few minutes they whispered among themselves. Then old Chief Skimmy rose and spoke for them all. "We are good

Apaches. We are peaceful. We are happy. It is the duty of good Apaches to punish bad Apaches. We will go with you and do as you tell us."

When John Clum and his Apache police reached the Cochise reservation they found the Indians in a state of wild excitement. In a plot to seize control of the tribe and lead it on the warpath, two subchiefs, turned outlaws, had tried to murder Cochise's sons. Natche, the younger son, had killed his attacker. Tahzay, the elder son, had only wounded the other, who had escaped to Mexico, taking his followers with him. Geronimo had stayed behind. He had a job to do.

With the tribe divided and fighting among themselves, Clum thought it best to transfer them all to San Carlos where his police could control them. Tahzay and Natche agreed, and the transfer was planned for the next morning. Then a boy came to Clum's camp, saying that Geronimo would like to talk to the white chief from San Carlos.

Clum knew Geronimo's reputation as a treacherous murderer. He agreed to the meeting, but was careful to station policemen close by with cocked rifles. Yet if an angel had walked into his camp, John Clum could not have been more surprised when Geronimo appeared. He was smiling, quiet-spoken, and seemed frightened. He said he was afraid of the outlaw subchief who had tried to kill his friend Tahzay. He and his people wanted nothing but peace and friendship. They would like to go to San Carlos and live as brothers with the white chief, but they couldn't be ready by morning. Their wikiup village was many miles away, and their horses were scattered in mountain pastures. If the white chief would wait three suns, he would bring all his people in, and they would go with him to San Carlos.

Clum shook Geronimo's hand and agreed gladly. Here, he thought, was another case of a good Indian being given a bad reputation by white men who had misunderstood and mistreated him. Clum made camp and settled down for his three-day wait.

The next morning, old people, women and children began drifting into Clum's camp. They said their men were gathering the horses and would be in after two more suns. With each sunrise more and more Apaches came in, but there were no warriors among them. By the fourth sunrise the camp was thronged, but Tahzay, Natche and a few sleepy peaceful warriors were the only men among them. Food was running low and it was time to begin the long march to San Carlos. Clem sent Beauford with a few trackers to find Geronimo's camp and tell the warriors to hurry along.

They had no trouble in finding the camp. It was only three miles away. But it had been stripped of everything that could be taken on a quick dash into the mountains of Mexico. Geronimo had completely outwitted John Clum.

He had needed three days, free from interference by the Apache police, to stir the warriors into an uprising. Now, with their dependents passed over to the United States government for support, they were ready for the warpath.

No bloodier or more terrible warpath was ever known than the one Geronimo and the outlaws followed for the next nine months. From their stronghold in the Sierra Madre Mountains they made countless raids into Arizona, killing, looting and burning. Also, hundreds upon hundreds of horses and cattle were stolen in Arizona and driven across the line into Mexico. Geronimo led some of the raids himself, but every one of them had the mark of his planning on it. Fresh troops of cavalry were rushed into Arizona, and the commanding general was ordered to capture Geronimo at any cost.

Month after month the outlaws knifed across the boundary in lightning-fast raids. Several times a band led by Geronimo ambushed a cavalry unit that was hot on its trail. The Indians would kill a few soldiers, then dash back across the line with a herd of stolen horses or cattle. Again, Geronimo was showing his contempt for American soldiers, goading them into a fury and committing some of his worst crimes almost within their sight.

At every report of a raid the cavalry units dashed away to trap and capture the renegades. They might as well have been chasing rainbows. Renegade scouts with powerful glasses watched them from high lookout points, smoke signals rose, and the outlaws knew every move the soldiers made. As the months went on, Geronimo grew more daring and insolent. Not a renegade was killed or captured, but the cavalrymen and their mounts were worn to exhaustion. Then the raiding suddenly stopped.

CHAPTER 18

THE ONLY CAPTURE
OF GERONIMO

GERONIMO, NOW NEARLY FIFTY YEARS OF AGE, HAD learned the ways of the white men and had decided to put the renegades into business. Settlers were pouring into the Rio Grande Valley of New Mexico. They would need horses for their spring work and cattle for their pastures. If the price were low enough they would ask no questions about the source of the stock. This had been Geronimo's reason for the great raids on Arizona livestock. He had more than two thousand stolen horses and cattle hiding in the mountains of Mexico, and it was time for the sales campaign to get under way.

The great herd was moved eastward so carefully that no white man saw it. Ten troops of cavalry were still hunting for Geronimo and the renegades in Arizona when the outlaws drove their herd back in to the United States, just west of El Paso, Texas.

Geronimo was a star salesman, and his judgment of the New Mexico settlers proved to be right. They were so greedy for cheap horses and cattle that they asked no questions. Of course, they knew the livestock had been stolen, and they also knew that it would be taken away from them if the government found out about it. So they were careful that no word reached the army posts. Geronimo had sold most of the herd, and the renegades were moving toward the Warm Springs Reservation when they were accidentally discovered by a cavalryman returning from a furlough.

Geronimo was number one on the Army's list of wanted criminals. There would be great glory for the general who was able to capture him, and disgrace for the one who tried and failed. Every general who had ever tried had failed, so none of them was anxious to tackle the job again. It was therefore passed on to the War Department at Washington. The War Department didn't want the job either, so it passed it along to the Commissioner of Indian Affairs.

On March 20, 1877, the Commissioner wired John Clum: "Take your Indian police and arrest renegade Indians at

Ojo Caliente (Warm Springs) New Mexico. . . . Remove renegades to San Carlos and hold them in confinement for murder and robbery. Call on military for aid if needed."

Clum had no idea how many renegades might be at Warm Springs, but this would be no mere police action. If cornered, the renegades would fight like wildcats. Apache would be pitted in battle against Apache if the San Carlos Indian police were used. This should not be done without the approval of the Apache court.

Clum called the members of his court together, interpreted the telegram to them, pointed out the danger and asked for their decision. After a few minutes of whispering, Chief Skimmy rose to give the decision: The Apaches wanted to govern themselves. To do so, good Apaches must fight bad Apaches if necessary. The police would go and arrest Geronimo and the renegades, but they wanted no help from the soldiers.

There were no mounts at San Carlos, and it was more than four hundred miles to Warm Springs, over arid deserts and rugged mountains. Clum issued two weeks' scant rations to his police and set out at once. Forty miles from Warm Springs he made camp and sent a few picked scouts ahead. They brought back word that a hundred renegades were camped three miles from the agency buildings. They were armed with repeating rifles, seemed to be expecting an attack, and had sentinels posted far out in all directions with powerful field glasses. Three subchiefs were in command, but Geronimo was doing the planning. If he learned that a strong police force was coming he would make a dash for the Mexican mountains, massacring whites as he went.

There seemed only one chance for success: Clum must reach Warm Springs in daylight with so small a force that Geronimo would have contempt for it. Leaving Beauford to follow slowly, Clum hurried ahead with Chief Skimmy and twenty members of the police. Early in the afternoon they marched boldly up to the Warm Springs agency buildings. This maneuver completely deceived Geronimo. He called in the renegade sentinels and the camp prepared for a fight.

The parade ground at Warm Springs was nearly square in shape. Office buildings faced it to the west, a long warehouse formed the south line, and a deep canyon cut it off to the north and east. With careful attention to the layout, Clum and Skimmy made plans for attempting the arrest. After dark they sent a messenger to carry the plans back to Clay Beauford.

At the first streak of dawn, another messenger was sent to tell Geronimo and the subchiefs that Agent Clum wanted to see them at the agency office. The outlaws were not only ready but waiting. As the sun rose, they strode arrogantly onto the parade grounds. Behind them crowded a hundred warriors with rifles ready. There was nothing to arouse their suspicions. Clum stood on the agency porch with five members of his police force near him. At each side of the building eight others were posted, equally spaced along the grounds.

As soon as the renegade warriors were in position, Geronimo strutted up to the porch where Clum stood waiting. Close behind him pressed the three subchiefs. They stared at the young agent with the utmost insolence. Clum looked straight in Geronimo's eyes and spoke to him in the Apache language. "You have broken Cochise's peace treaty, killed many white men, and stolen their horses and cattle. Now the Apache police and I have come with orders from Washington to take you and these outlaw warriors to the San Carlos Reservation."

Geronimo stepped closer and shouted into Clum's face, "You talk very brave, but we do not like that kind of talk! We are not going to San Carlos with you, and unless you are very careful, you and your Apache police will not go back either. Your bodies will stay here to make food for the coyotes."

Clum raised a finger to his hat, and the warehouse doors flew open. Seventy-eight Apache policemen raced out, two paces apart, each with his rifle cocked and his finger on the trigger. They did not run toward the massed renegades, but skirted the parade grounds. Before the startled outlaws realized what was happening, they were completely surrounded.

Geronimo was carrying a United States Army rifle. As

the police broke from the warehouse his hand flashed to the trigger. But when he looked up for his target he was staring into the muzzles of twenty-one Apache police rifles. His hand dropped away.

Displaying his great acting ability, Geronimo appeared to accept his defeat. All sign of anger left his face and voice. He smiled and said, *"Enju* (it is well)! We have been on the warpath a long time and are tired. If you want to have a big smoke and big talk we are ready."

Geronimo stood quietly while Clum stepped down and took the rifle. Then the Indian's free hand moved cautiously toward the knife in his belt. A policeman, leaping forward, snatched it away. Others sprang to disarm the subchiefs. With their leaders disarmed, the renegade warriors became bewildered. The Apache police began closing in. The shock of being surrounded by cocked rifles in the hands of their own people was too much for even the bravest renegades. Slowly they laid their arms on the ground, and the Apache police herded them into a corner of the parade grounds.

Leg irons were fastened on Geronimo and the three subchiefs, and they were put in a guarded stockade. But the disarmed warriors were allowed to return to their camp and prepare for the long march to San Carlos. They had seen the loyalty and efficiency of the Apache police, and they gave no further trouble. Geronimo and the subchiefs, still in irons, were taken to San Carlos in a wagon; the other prisoners were marched afoot.

On arriving to San Carlos, Geronimo, the subchiefs and fourteen warriors who could be proved guilty of murdering white men were put into the guardhouse. Clum wired the Commissioner of Indian Affairs at once, telling him that the mission was completed. He then notified the civil authorities at Tucson that he was ready to turn the prisoners over to them for trial. He also sent word that his Apache police would furnish evidence to prove each of the prisoners guilty of murder.

Thus, John Clum executed his mission bravely and brilliantly. But no matter how brave and brilliant a man may be, he cannot long succeed alone. John Clum had succeeded wonderfully in making friends of Apaches, controlling them and teaching them to be good citizens. In stopping the Tucson Ring from robbing them, he had succeeded where General Crook had failed. In capturing Geronimo and the renegades, he had succeeded where other generals and more than two thousand United States cavalrymen had failed.

But John P. Clum was not a man to hide his light under a bushel. From the time of his arrival in Arizona he had made no white friends, though he had made many enemies by bragging of the fine job he had done. Army officers had disliked him from the beginning. Now his loud boasts of having captured Geronimo where they had failed made them his bitter enemies. None of them wanted him to have the credit for capturing Geronimo and breaking up the Apache outlaw gangs. They joined with the Tucson Ring and forced his resignation as agent of San Carlos.

Within two weeks after Clum left San Carlos, Geronimo and the other prisoners were released, given new blankets and turned loose on the reservation. This was too much for Clay Beauford; he quit as chief of the Apache police.

CHAPTER 19

GERONIMO'S
FIRST SURRENDER

THE NEW AGENT AT SAN CARLOS DISBANDED THE Apache court and the Indian police lost interest. The Tucson Ring again took control and quickly began robbing the Apaches. Food rations were cut almost to the starvation point and no clothing was issued.

This was just what Geronimo wanted. This, he believed, would give him a chance to stir the whole Apache nation into an uprising. He could now become its one great chief. He went from end to end of the reservation, talking, pleading, shouting and trying to stir the warriors into going on the warpath. His oratory was entirely wasted. The Apaches wanted to live in peace, and they knew that

Geronimo's raiding and treachery had been responsible for most of their trouble. They preferred to live as best they could on the reservation rather than to follow him.

Until arrested by the Apache police, Geronimo had turned his hatred against only the Americans and Mexicans. Now it was also turned against any Apache who opposed him. He gathered a few of the fiercest subchiefs and warriors who had been among the arrested renegades. In a bold raid on the agency they stole great quantities of guns and ammunition. Then, taking the best horses on the reservation, they made a dash into the Mexican mountains. Hoo was still there with more than a hundred outlaw warriors—and Geronimo had a plan in mind. He would drive the Apaches off the reservation if he could not lead them off.

By this time Hoo had become a drunken good-for-nothing. Geronimo had no trouble in getting him to join the plot. But the attack on the reservation was a complete failure. The Apache police fought like demons, driving Geronimo and his outlaws back into Mexico.

In revenge Geronimo led another raid on San Carlos. He and a few followers sneaked onto the reservation at night, killing the new chief and six of the Apache police. Then they raced back across the border before the soldiers could catch them. These two raids did Geronimo a great deal of harm. The reservation Apaches hated and feared him more than ever. And Geronimo's cruelty toward his own people turned Chato, the most brilliant among the renegade subchiefs, against him.

Yet, though the other renegades would not accept Geronimo as their chief, they followed him on the warpath. For four years he terrorized northern Mexico and southern Arizona with blood and fire. Two Mexican armies and 3,000 United States cavalrymen took the field against him, but neither he nor his raiders were so much as scratched. With each passing year his contempt for soldiers became greater. He even raided a United States Army post to steal guns and ammunition.

With the Tucson Ring robbing the reservation Indians ruthlessly, even the most peaceful among the Apaches were forced to raid the whites to keep their families from starvation. By 1882 Indian raids in Arizona had become so unbearable that the citizens rebelled. They demanded that the government send more soldiers and that every Apache be killed. This led to President Arthur's discovery of the Tucson Ring's thievery and the commanding general's inability to control Indians.

The President and Congress took immediate action. A treaty was made with Mexico, allowing the soldiers of either nation to cross the International Boundary when in pursuit of renegade Indians. General Crook was transferred back to Arizona, an honest agent was put in charge of San Carlos, and the leaders of the Tucson Ring were brought to trial.

When General Crook returned to Arizona he found less than a thousand Apaches on the reservation. The rest were scattered far and wide. Some had gone to join the outlaws in Mexico; others were hidden away in the mountains, raiding the whites for a living. Wasting no time, General Crook went alone to hunt out the old chiefs and subchiefs who had known and trusted him. Through them he sent word to every Apache band. Those who returned to the reservation would not be punished, and would be protected and fed. Any who failed to return would be tracked down and severely punished.

The General's reputation for honesty and fair dealing was a byword among the Apaches who had known him. They rapidly spread the news of his return. The raiding stopped, and the people began pouring back onto the reservation. Now General Crook could turn his attention to Geronimo and the outlaws.

Experience had taught the General that white soldiers could not run down and catch Apache warriors in rough mountain country. The job would require other Apaches with the necessary cunning, strength and endurance. It would be risky for a few white officers to take a company of armed Apache warriors into wild country, particularly for the capture of other Apaches. But the risk would have to be taken if the renegades were to be captured.

The General sent out word that he would accept Apache volunteers for enlistment in a company to be known as the

Apache Scouts. All of John Clum's old police force and many other fine young warriors volunteered. Some of them had been outlaws at one time or another, but they all despised Geronimo and were anxious to help with his capture. Each took the oath of allegiance to the United States, and not one of them ever broke it. They were formed into a company with Captain Crawford, Lieutenant Gatewood and Lieutenant Davis as officers, and Al Sieber as chief of scouts. Each was a superb athlete and had the ability to win the confidence of the Indians.

The Sierra Madre Mountains extend two hundred miles south of the Mexican line and they are a hundred miles wide. They rise to heights of more than two miles, and are cut by deep impassable canyons. The Apache outlaws had established their stronghold in these mountains, and no white man had ever been able to force his way into it.

With only one troop of cavalry, but with one hundred and ninety-three Apache scouts and two large pack trains, General Crook entered Mexico in April 1883. By early May he had reached the summit of the Sierra Madres. The country he had crossed was so rugged that several pack mules fell from narrow trails high on the canyon walls. His cavalry was completely exhausted, and his mules had nearly reached the limit of their endurance. But the Apache scouts were as fresh as ever, and their officers were all in good shape. The General decided he must establish a central supply camp and carry on his campaign with small scouting bands.

For a week no trace of the renegades was discovered. Then the scouts came upon an outlaw camp. The warriors were all away on raids, but a few women were captured and taken to General Crook. From these he learned that Hoo was dead. Geronimo had tried to take over as chief, but only a few of the warriors would follow him. Chato had become his bitter enemy, and the renegades were now split into half a dozen bands, each with a subchief leader. Moreover, all the leaders were worried by the fact that General Crook had been able to enlist Apaches against them. They could escape white soldiers in these high mountains, but, hampered by dependents, they could not hope to escape Apache scouts.

General Crook released the women on their promise to act as messengers. They were to take word to every outlaw leader that the scouts would be kept hot on their trail until they and all their people had come in and surrendered.

Next day Chato came in and surrendered, but it soon became evident that all the other renegade leaders were letting Geronimo do their scheming. Old men, women and children began to drift into General Crook's camp, crying, "Surrender! Surrender!" They all seemed half starved, and they begged for food and fell upon the army rations greedily. Before the end of the second day, three hundred and twenty-five of these refugees had come in. Only fifty-two were men, and thirty-nine of these were either crippled or too old to fight.

Near sunset Geronimo and the other band leaders came in under the flag of truce. Geronimo was not strutting nor was he arrogant. He was on his best behavior, and spoke as if he were chief of all the Apaches. For hours he talked about the wrongs the Americans had done his people— most of it straight from his imagination. Then he offered to surrender, but only on his own terms:

He and his people must not be disarmed or punished for their past sins. They must be met at the boundary by American soldiers, protected on their way to San Carlos, given new blankets and clothing, and kept supplied with plenty of food. If these conditions were granted, he would gather his widely scattered family and bring them to the border at the end of two moons.

General Crook had clearly been outwitted. Geronimo had known him to be an honest man, and had used his honesty against him. The General could have ordered Geronimo and the other leaders seized and made prisoners, but he could not have done it honestly. They had not been captured, but had come to his camp under a flag of truce. It would be treachery to lay a hand on them. Beyond this, the renegades had now freed themselves of their dependents and burdened the General with them. His supplies were nearly exhausted and it was impossible for him to continue his campaign. He had no choice but to accept

Geronimo's terms and get out of the mountains before his own situation became desperate.

One by one the leaders brought their bands to the boundary and were escorted to San Carlos, but there was no sign of Geronimo. Month after month passed. The War Department criticized General Crook severely for letting Geronimo slip through his fingers. The Arizona newspapers demanded that the General be replaced and that all the Apaches be moved to some reservation in the East. The reservation Apaches realized that their welfare was being seriously harmed by Geronimo's actions. Medicine men performed long ceremonies, calling down evil upon his head and pleading with Usen to strike him dead or bring him in.

Following his surrender Chato had become a model Indian and a devoted admirer of General Crook. Now he went to the General, offering to take his own Indian warriors into Mexico to kill or capture Geronimo. The General, of course, could not agree to it. Under the treaty with Mexico, United States forces could cross the boundary only when hot on the trail of renegade Indians, and there was now no hot trail. All that could be done was to keep soldiers stationed along the American side of the boundary.

In March 1884, Geronimo arrived at the boundary driving a heard of 350 stolen Mexican cattle. There were only fifteen warriors in his band, accompanied by seventy women and children. He was isolated and ugly, loudly demanding to know why the soldiers were trying to interfere with him. (Of course, the cattle he had stolen were all fat, and it was clear that he had brought them for sale to the Arizona settlers.) When Geronimo found himself outnumbered and surrounded he switched his position quickly. He demanded that, under the terms of his old surrender, he and his band be escorted to San Carlos. And he insisted that the cattle be moved slowly so they would lose no weight.

Geronimo's greed did him little good. As soon as he reached the reservation the cattle were taken from him and turned over to the agency for beef. Their Mexican owners were paid for them. Geronimo was furious at this loss, and devoted himself to causing all the trouble he could on the reservation.

CHAPTER 20

THE LAST GERONIMO
OUTBREAK

JUST AS THEY HAD DONE UNDER JOHN CLUM, THE Apaches settled down to live contentedly under the fair and honest treatment of General Crook. They respected, admired and trusted him as their friend. He set up a separate camp for all those who had been renegades, placed only one white officer, Lieutenant Davis, in charge of them, and let them govern themselves. The Apache scouts were reduced to a small force which took the place of Clum's Apache police, and Chato was appointed sergeant. This was the highest position held by any Apache and Chato took great pride in it. Under his watchful eye wrongdoers were punished quickly, and even those who had been the most savage renegades were soon living peacefully.

Geronimo was the only exception. He was still determined to become chief of all the Apaches and to lead them on the warpath against the Americans. Time and again he laid plots which he believed would start uprisings, but each time Chato and Lieutenant Davis discovered these plots and broke them up. With each failure Geronimo's hatred for Chato and Lieutenant Davis increased, but the number of Apaches who would listen to his oratory became fewer.

Geronimo could still perform all the rituals he had learned in his early training as a medicine man. When his oratory failed he tried to frighten the Apaches by using these rituals. He bragged that the power of his medicine was so strong no enemy had ever been able to catch or harm him. He claimed great influence with the evil spirits, threatening to bring down sickness and death upon any Apache who would not follow him.

It was true that Geronimo seemed to have a charmed life, and that ill fortune had befallen many of his enemies. Any other man with such a record could certainly have gathered an enormous following among the superstitious Apaches. But Geronimo's reputation as a liar and troublemaker had become too great. By the time he had been back on the reservation a year, his followers had shrunk to half a dozen warriors. Unfortunately, three of them were important men among the Apaches. One was Natche, the son of Cochise. Another was Mangas, son of

Mangas Coloradas. The third was Chihuahua, once a powerful and ruthless subchief.

Natche and Mangas were brave, truthful and honest. All the Apaches liked and trusted them. But both had fallen under Geronimo's spell. They were convinced that he was a holy man, that he could speak with the spirits and influence them, and that everything he said about his power was true.

Geronimo finally realized that he could never start an uprising by himself. It would have to be done by men whom the Apaches trusted and would follow. And what better men could be found than Natche and Mangas? Chihuahua would be useful, too. A known murderer, he was not very smart, and would do anything he believed the spirits had directed. He was just the right man to use as a cat's-paw (a person used by another to gain an end).

Very carefully Geronimo laid a master plot which he believed would frighten all the Apaches into an outbreak. He thought he had planned it so carefully that no suspicion of guilt could fall on him in case it failed. It would also let him vent his hatred of Chato and Lieutenant Davis.

Night after night he sat with Natche and Mangas, performing his rituals, pretending to go into trances and whispering messages that he claimed to have received from the spirits. He told them the Apaches were in terrible danger. The white men wanted them all killed. Right now General Crook was massing thousands of cavalrymen just outside the reservation, waiting for anything that would give him an excuse to begin the killing. The Apaches must tread softly and do nothing that could cause the slightest trouble. If it should start, their only hope would be in a sudden dash for the Mexican mountains. Word of this danger must be spread quickly and quietly to all the people.

While Natche and Mangas were spreading news of this great danger, Geronimo whispered quite different messages to Chihuahua. He said the spirits had told him that Chato was a traitor and the greatest enemy of the Apaches. He was scheming with Lieutenant Davis to have Chihuahua and several of the other leaders killed or imprisoned. Both Chato and Davis must be murdered quickly if the leaders were to be saved.

Chihuahua believed Geronimo, but didn't dare to commit the murders himself. This Geronimo had expected, and he had made his plans accordingly. Two of Chihuahua's nephews were in Chato's company of scouts, and would do anything their uncle told them to. Geronimo had Chihuahua call them in and give them careful instructions.

At dawn Chato often marched the scouts to Lieutenant Davis's tent, where they were paraded in ranks for inspection. At the next inspection the nephews were to take places in the rear rank. As Lieutenant Davis came from his tent they were to step back out of rank with their rifles leveled. At the same moment one was to shoot Chato and the other, Lieutenant Davis. When he heard the shots Chihuahua was to run to Natche and Mangas, shouting that the scouts had mutinied and killed Lieutenant Davis and Chato, and that General Crook was coming with the soldiers.

Geronimo felt sure that Natche and Mangas, as soon as they heard the news, would frighten the whole camp into making a dash for Mexico. His greatest worry was that Chihuahua might not hear the shots, so he had his own son hidden near Lieutenant Davis's tent. At the moment of the murders he was to run to Chihuahua with the news.

As had so often happened before, Chato suspected the plot. When Chihuahua's nephew stepped back and raised their rifles they found themselves covered, lost their nerve and ran for their lives. At the same instant, Geronimo's son raced to his father with word that the plot had failed.

Geronimo was furiously angry but still determined to stampede the Apaches into an outbreak. He ran to Natche and Mangas, wildly waving his arms and screaming that Lieutenant Davis and Chato had been murdered, and that General Crook was close at hand with the soldiers. Every Apache would be killed to avenge the murders.

Natche and Mangas leaped on their horses and whipped them toward the south, shouting the horrible alarm as they rode. Chihuahua and Geronimo dashed away with their families, yelling wildly to the people to mount and follow them before the soldiers arrived. A hundred frightened women and children were stampeded by the excitement. They mounted any pony they could catch and fled southward in panic. But only thirty warriors and eight boys old enough to bear arms joined in the outbreak.

The rest of the Apaches knew that Geronimo had cast his spell over Natche, Mangas and Chihuahua, and they recognized this as a Geronimo plot. Of course, they could not know so quickly that Lieutenant Davis and Chato had not been harmed, but they did know General Crook. They could not believe he would kill innocent Indians to avenge a Geronimo crime.

The renegades were barely off the reservation when Chihuahua's nephews came racing to overtake them, shouting that Chato and Lieutenant Davis were hot on their trail with the Apache scouts. This led to the discovery that the whole affair had been a Geronimo plot, and that Natche, Mangas and Chihuahua had been used as dupes. Mangas and Chihuahua were ready to kill Geronimo on the spot. It was only Natche's belief that he was a holy man that saved his life.

Both Mangas and Chihuahua wanted to turn back to the reservation at once, but neither of them could face the disgrace of having let Geronimo make a fool of him. Each rallied his own followers and raced with them toward the Mexican mountains, leaving Geronimo to follow with less than a dozen warriors and more than sixty frightened women and children.

CHAPTER 21

WOLF ON THE RUN

DURING THE YEAR GERONIMO WAS ON THE RESERVATION, there had been no Indian trouble in Arizona. But now the citizens again demanded that all the Apaches be removed from their territory and imprisoned in the East. Realizing that Geronimo was the sole cause of this demand, the Apaches were determined to find and kill him before he could stir up further trouble. Hundreds of warriors volunteered from every tribe on the reservation. Chato came forward with more than a hundred from the renegade camp. Every one of them had been an outlaw, but they all despised Geronimo, and they alone knew the renegade strongholds and hiding places in the Sierra Madres.

General Crook moved rapidly, reorganized the Apache scouts to full force and divided them into companies under Lieutenant Davis, Lieutenant Gatewood and Al Sieber. He placed Captain Crawford in command of an all-Apache campaign into Mexico. The General's only orders were, "Keep the scouts on the renegade trail until the outlaws are killed, captured, or driven to unconditional surrender."

Chato blamed himself for failing to discover Geronimo's plot in time to stop the outbreak and save his friends Natche and Mangas from disgrace. He and his band of scouts took up the renegade trail and followed it like bloodhounds. At the place where Chihuahua and Mangas had threatened to kill Geronimo, Chato read the story from tracks on the ground as easily as we could read it on a printed page. He had no interest in the trails of the Chihuahua or Mangas bands, but swore he'd run down Geronimo if it took the rest of his life.

Geronimo's trail to the Mexican border was as easy for the scouts to follow as an open road. The tracks showed that he had driven the women and children mercilessly. In the whole distance of 150 miles, he had not let them stop for food, water or rest. The weaker ponies had given out and died by the way, but he had doubled the people onto stronger horses and raced on.

Soon after reaching the Sierra Madres, the trail led onto a bare, rocky mountain—and disappeared. Geronimo had wrapped his horses' hoofs in skins, and had covered the trail so expertly that even the best Apache scouts could not find it. A month passed and hundreds of square miles of mountains were scoured without picking up a trace. Then Chato discovered footprints leading to a hidden camp. It was surrounded, and fifteen women and children were captured in a running battle. But Chato's scouts were on foot, and by this time Geronimo had mounted his followers on fresh, swift horses, scattered his band widely and slipped away.

Captain Crawford established a central supply camp in the heart of the Sierra Madres and spread scouting bands in every direction. Chato scouted every renegade hideout and stronghold within a hundred miles, but the only signs found were of Mangas' and Chihuahua's people. These signs showed that both bands were afoot, nearly exhausted, and that their leaders had moved them far to the south.

For another month it seemed that Geronimo and his band had disappeared into thin air. Then a fresh trail was picked up and the whole band was trapped on a mountaintop. Two warriors were killed in a running battle, but Geronimo split his band and once more slipped out of the trap.

Week followed disappointing week before the new renegade camp was discovered and surrounded. Just when capture seemed assured, Geronimo led a wild charge straight through the surrounding circle of scouts.

Three more of his warriors were killed and another fifteen women and children captured, but Geronimo raced on— leading his well-mounted band into the highest and roughest part of the mountains.

By this time food and ammunition were running dangerously low. Captain Crawford was obliged to withdraw a large part of his force and go to Fort Bowie for supplies. He called in all the scouts, asked Chato to select forty of the best, and issued them what rations he could spare. Placing Lieutenant Davis and Al Sieber in charge, the Captain ordered them to pick up Geronimo's trail and stick to it as long as their rations lasted. They were then to make their way out of the mountains as best they could.

Now the greatest game of hide-and-seek in all history began. All day and through the night the scouts stuck to the trail, keeping up the steady Apache trot that could eventually wear down the endurance of any horse. But Geronimo was watching his back trail with powerful glasses, and he drove his band ruthlessly.

At the end of three days the scouts were entirely out of rations. They had hardly stopped for an hour's rest and had not yet sighted a single renegade. Although Lieutenant Davis and Al Sieber were superb athletes, the pace of the scouts had been too much for them and they were nearly exhausted. They believed the chase was hopeless and must be abandoned, but Chato and the scouts would not give up. Geronimo had proved himself the enemy of his own people—and his own people would settle with him. Besides, the pace was telling on the renegade band; dead horses were beginning to mark the trail. Meat had been stripped from them and wolfed down raw as the band continued its flight.

Geronimo was not running blindly; he was driving to reach the Rain Mountains before he was overtaken. On the fourth morning, with the renegades less than two hours ahead of the scouts, the rains began. A sudden shower washed out the trail. Lieutenant Davis fanned the scouts into a front twenty miles wide. They ranged back and forth to check every canyon or hiding place and drive the renegades eastward, out of the rain belt. Day after day the rains continued. Time and again a trail was picked up, only to be lost in another deluge. For every mile they drove the renegades, the scouts had to cover at least five, but Chato gave them no rest.

Lieutenant Davis and Al Sieber were traveling less than a third of the distance covered by their constantly ranging scouts, but the two men were in far worse condition. Their shoes and clothing were torn to shreds, their backs sunburned and blistered, and their bleeding feet had swollen to double their normal size. For two weeks their only food had been roots and a few berries. But they were slowly driving Geronimo out of the rain belt; and stuck doggedly to the task.

By the end of the seventeenth day Geronimo had been driven onto the eastern slope of the Sierra Madres. Next morning Chato found a clearly marked trail, read it and reported to Lieutenant Davis. Geronimo had gathered his band soon after dark and was making a run for the nearest settlement. He would now have a lead of several hours, but his people were in a very bad shape. They had eaten all their horses and must be nearing starvation. The feet of the women and children were bleeding badly. All camp equipment, blankets and extra clothing had been abandoned. In a hard day's drive the scouts would be able to overtake and capture them.

Lieutenant Davis, Al Sieber and the scouts ran without rest until late in the afternoon. Then, from a mountaintop, the renegades were sighted. But Geronimo had raided a settlement. His people were mounted on fresh horses and traveling rapidly.

The next three days showed the stuff Davis and Sieber were made of. With their feet bleeding at every step, they ran 125 miles. By that time the steady trot of the scouts had worn down Geronimo's horses and cut his lead to four miles. Chato drove the scouts forward to make the capture before nightfall—but it was never made.

When the exhausted renegades were only a mile ahead, a force of Mexican cavalry came racing up to Lieutenant Davis from the rear. Its colonel wanted credit for capturing the famous Geronimo and insisted that

Lieutenant Davis call off his scouts. Being in Mexican territory, the Lieutenant had no choice but to abandon the chase. And, as was always the case, Geronimo slipped away from the Mexican soldiers during the first night.

CHAPTER 22

GERONIMO AND THE
EVIL SPIRITS

DURING THE NEXT FOUR MONTHS CAPTAIN CRAWFORD and the scouts combed countless square miles of Mexican mountains without finding so much as a renegade's footprint. But Geronimo was certainly in the Sierra Madres and up to his old tricks. Vicious raids and murders, committed at a dozen widely scattered places, bore the unmistakable mark of Geronimo's cruelty.

The Mexican government released hundreds of convicts from prisons, forming them into companies of soldiers known as Irregulars. They were furnished with arms, supplies and a few Indian guides, and then sent into the mountains to run down and kill the renegades. These Irregulars were cowardly soldiers. They tried to avoid rather than to find the renegades. By hiding out, they could live in luxury on government supplies.

On New Year's Day, 1886, Chato picked up a renegade trail high in the mountains. He studied it carefully and reported to Captain Crawford that Geronimo had stolen many horses and joined his band with Chihuahua's. They were heading for the Devil's Backbone, the highest, wildest and coldest part of the Sierra Madres. Chato was sure that Geronimo planned to hole up where the weather was too severe for scouts to follow him afoot.

The risk of being trapped by blizzards and frozen in those high mountains was great, but Chato and the scouts urged that the trail be followed quickly. Otherwise it would be entirely lost in the blowing snow. Captain Crawford fully realized the danger; he would not have ordered the scouts to take such a risk. However, since they were anxious to go, he determined to keep Geronimo on the run until he was killed or captured. The Captain took personal command of the dangerous mission and chose Lieutenant Maus, his most rugged young officer, as his second in command.

Moving only by night, and with Chato and a few picket scouts far out ahead, Captain Crawford picked up the renegade trail and stuck to it doggedly. The mountains were extremely high and rough, and the temperature was well below zero. Over and over, the trail was lost in blizzard, but each time the scouts picked it up again and drove ahead.

For nine days and nights Captain Crawford, Lieutenant Maus and the thinly clothed scouts suffered horribly. Hands, feet and ears were frostbitten, and eyelids swelled nearly shut, but no one would give up the chase. Then, soon after dark, the advance scouts sent back word that they had discovered Geronimo's camp. It was pitched in a deep gorge and no sentries were posted. Every sign showed that Geronimo believed he was perfectly safe and had holed up in a permanent winter camp.

Planning to make a surprise attack before dawn, Captain Crawford pushed his scouts to the utmost. All night they fought their way forward through a howling storm—scaling cliffs, wading icy streams and dropping down rock walls into deep canyons. But the going was too rough for the endurance of any white man. Captain Crawford and Lieutenant Maus could make the last few miles only with a scout helping them at each side.

With the first gray of dawn Captain Crawford had the scouts spread in an almost complete circle around the sleeping camp. The gorge was in pitch-blackness. The sharpest human ear could not pick up a sound as the scouts drew their circle closer. Suddenly, from the depths of the gorge, a burro brayed. Geronimo had used the tattle-tale trick from his boyhood days in the horse camps.

Surprise was no longer possible. Captain Crawford shouted for the scouts to rush the camp. The few minutes it took them to scramble down the walls was time enough for the renegades to get away. Leaping on their horses, the outlaws raced out of the gorge and scattered in every direction. It would have been useless to try following them in the darkness.

For months Geronimo had been raiding in preparation for his winter's hole-up, but he had been forced to abandon everything in his sudden flight. Hundreds of Mexican blankets, many rifles, great quantities of ammunition, warm clothing, and tons of dried meat were found in the camp. The renegades might eat their horses to keep from starving, but they could not live to get out of those high mountains without blankets and warm clothing.

Captain Crawford and the scouts spent the whole day in burning and destroying the plunder in the renegade wikiups. Soon after dark an old Apache woman sneaked into camp, waving a white cloth as a flag of truce. She said Geronimo had sent her to say that he and his people wanted only to be taken back to the reservation where they could live in peace. He would come in at once with all his warriors, and would surrender on any terms the white chief of the soldiers wanted.

Captain Crawford knew Geronimo well enough to suspect an ambush. In the darkness, that deep gorge would be an ideal place for it. The Captain was anxious for the surrender, but would meet Geronimo and his outlaws only in an open canyon where there was no chance for ambush. He sent back word that any renegade who tried to enter his camp during the night would be killed. If Geronimo wished to surrender unconditionally, he would meet him the next morning in an open canyon two miles to the north.

The happenings of the next morning almost seemed to prove Geronimo's boast that he had influence with the evil spirits. No one could have guessed that any human being except the renegades were within fifty miles. But when Captain Crawford led his scouts toward the canyon where he was to meet Geronimo, they suddenly came upon a camp of Mexican Irregulars.

Realizing there might be trouble, Captain Crawford leaped onto a high rock, shouting in Spanish that the scouts were American soldiers. He was still shouting when a soldier raised his gun and fired. The bullet hit Captain Crawford in the head, fatally wounding but not killing him. As he fell, the Apache scouts rushed up to avenge him. The Irregulars ran, but for a few minutes their Indian guides fought like demons.

While the unfortunate battle was going on, Geronimo lay watching in glee from his hiding place in a side canyon. His medicine was still strong! The evil spirits had come to his rescue! Now any surrender would be on his own terms. A junior officer would not carry on the chase and let his captain die without trying to get him to a doctor. And with Mexican Irregulars in the mountains, there would be food and clothing for the renegades. One Apache war whoop would put these cowardly soldiers to rout, leaving their well-stocked camp to be plundered.

While Lieutenant Maus sat grieving and holding his dying captain's head in his lap, Geronimo strutted boldly into camp, waiving a flag of truce. The surrender terms he demanded were those of a conqueror rather than a defeated outlaw.

Had Lieutenant Maus followed General Crook's orders, he would have told Geronimo to return to the warpath, and would have set the scouts hot on his trail. In that way, the Irregulars' camp would not have been plundered, and the renegades would quickly have been forced into unconditional surrender. But Geronimo had reasoned shrewdly. Captain Crawford was still breathing, and Lieutenant Maus was anxious to get him to a doctor quickly. He also wanted to keep any hold he could on the renegades. He pleaded with Geronimo to come to Fort Bowie with him and talk terms of surrender with General Crook.

Geronimo was quick to take advantage of Lieutenant Maus' dilemma. He agreed to meet General Crook for a surrender talk, but only under three conditions: The meeting must be held in the Canyon of the Frauds, twenty miles south of the border, in two moons. General Crook must come without soldiers, and with only a few scouts and interpreters. In the meantime, the renegades must not be molested by either American soldiers or Apache scouts.

There was no hope of saving Captain Crawford's life, but in his eagerness and anxiety, Lieutenant Maus disobeyed General Crook's orders and agreed to Geronimo's terms. In honor, General Crook could do nothing but carry out the agreement made by his officer.

CHAPTER 23

THE WOLF, TURNED COYOTE

GERONIMO HAD BEEN VERY CRAFTY IN CHOOSING THE Canyon of the Frauds for his surrender talk with General Crook. It was the wildest place along the border of the Sierra Madres. Its deep gorge and jagged surrounding cliffs made it a perfect setting for an ambush. Long before General Crook and his party arrived, Geronimo hid the best marksmen of his band high along the canyon walls. From there they could cover the meeting ground with their rifles and quickly escape back into the high mountains.

Believing he had General Crook in his power, Geronimo

strutted into the meeting and demanded surrender terms more ridiculous than ever before: All his past sins and those of his followers must be forgiven. They were not to be disarmed or punished in any way. Instead, they were to be taken back to San Carlos Reservation, given new clothing and blankets, fed and allowed to do as they pleased.

General Crook realized that Geronimo had prepared an ambush for him, but he was not afraid. He knew that he held what Geronimo had always coveted but had never been able to gain—the trust of the leadership of the Apaches. With that trust, the General needed no soldiers to protect him or to enforce the surrender terms he would offer.

After Geronimo had made his demands, General Crook looked him calmly in the eyes and told him he could never return to the San Carlos Reservation. Neither he nor his followers had a single friend left among the Apaches. If he were taken back to the reservation he would surely be killed by his own people. The renegades might surrender if they wished. If they did, they would be treated as prisoners of war. Their lives would be spared, but they would be imprisoned in the East. If they did not choose to surrender they might turn to the warpath. In that case he would set Chato and the Apache scouts back on their trail.

Geronimo glanced quickly at the few scouts who had come with General Crook. In their faces, he read the truth of the General's words. Fright came into his eyes, his hands trembled, and he asked if he might have till morning to talk with his people and make up his mind.

Next morning, Geronimo came to General Crook's tent with Natche and Chihuahua. There was no strutting and demanding. He stood back, a beaten man, as Chihuahua and Natche stepped forward and surrendered. Then Geronimo, who might have been the Apaches' greatest chief if he had not been dishonest and greedy, stepped forward and mumbled, "What the others say I say also. I give myself up to you. Do with me what you please. I surrender."

General Crook returned to Fort Bowie and left Lieutenant Maus to come in with the surrendered renegades. Geronimo started with the others, but on the way his courage failed him. He could no longer face the hatred of his own people. Taking Natche and a few followers who still believed him to be a holy man, the wolf of the warpath sneaked back like a frightened coyote to hide in the vastness of the Sierra Madres. But now fear followed him even into the mountains.

With every man's hand raised against him, with all hope gone of ever becoming a leader of his people, Geronimo again surrendered within a few months. He, his band, and other Apaches who had been renegades, were imprisoned in Florida. After a few years they were moved to Alabama, and finally to a reservation at Fort Sill, Oklahoma. Year by year, Geronimo's bitterness and hatred increased. Whenever he found a chance he drowned his anger in whiskey.

In February 1909, when Geronimo was nearly eighty years old, he drove a horse and buggy from the Fort Sill Reservation to Lawton, Oklahoma. He carried with him a toy bow and arrows he had made, traded them for a bottle of whiskey and started back to the reservation. Part way home, he fell from the buggy in a drunken stupor. It was a cold, rainy night, and he was not found for several hours. A few days later he died of pneumonia.

While Geronimo cannot be honored as a hero, he will always stand as a landmark in American history. He was the last Indian leader who tried, through warfare, to turn back the tide of white civilization.

AFTERWORD

GERONIMO LIVED FOR OVER TWENTY-ONE YEARS AS A "prisoner with special privileges" of the United States government. He may have died unglamorously of pneumonia instead of battle wounds, but his last years were actually very symbolic of the transition that had taken place in the American West.

In captivity he became a celebrity of sorts. Even though he was always heavily guarded, he traveled extensively in his later years. He attended the St. Louis World's Fair in 1904 and rode in President Theodore Roosevelt's inaugural parade in 1905. While still alive, he became a living legend of the old West, and was the most famous Indian in the world, whose exploits were written about in many stories—some fact and some fiction.

To this day, Geronimo is considered a great hero by some for his unrelenting and fierce fight against the white man's encroachment on the Apache lands and their traditional way of life. There is no question that he was a great leader and a brilliant warrior who held both the United States and Mexican governments at bay for many years.

Others feel he was an uncontrolled and selfish renegade who used terror and violence to the detriment of his own people. For the last ten years of his struggle against the United States Army, his actions probably caused his own people much unnecessary suffering.

It has been well over a hundred years since he freely rampaged throughout the Southwest, and with the passing of the years, there is one thing that everyone can agree on—Geronimo is an important and colorful figure in American history. His determined efforts to fight for the independence of his people against great odds have come to symbolize the spirit of America.

THE EDITORS

Index